Outrageous Promotions That Are Outrageously Effective

Discover how to put the power of the $20 Billion dollar promotional products industry to easily and quickly flood your business with more prospects, clients and sales than you can handle without hiring an expensive marketing guru or an overpriced ad agency.

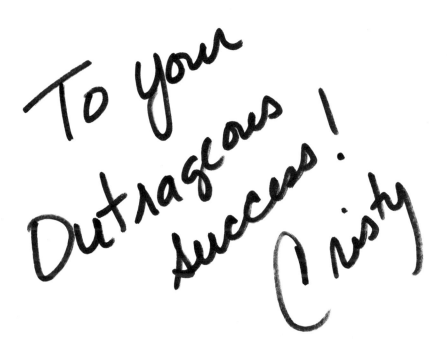

living
successful
interesting
to you

Author's Bio

Hi there, please give me a quick minute of your time to introduce myself, Robert Vico and my business partner and co-author Cristina Arce. We are entrepreneurs, authors, speakers and self-diagnosed "Marketing Junkies."

Since the age of 24 I've been an entrepreneur making it on my own and let me tell you it ain't easy! I've made it on my own as a small business owner for over two decades. And after that many years in business I can confidently say that…

"I hate selling….but I **LOVE** marketing!"

Now don't get me wrong selling products and services is how businesses make money. But the truth of the matter is that marketing is truly where the money is because nothing sells until you do the marketing.

Marketing always comes first…selling always comes second.

It took me a few years to learn that it's not the selling that makes money but rather using the power of marketing to get people to buy because the reality is that people hate to be sold but they sure do love to buy.

So back in 2000 I took over a bankrupt screen-printing business and put my aggressive no BS marketing approach to work and I was able to quickly turn that bankrupt business around and create it into a million dollar business.

That business has now transformed from a t-shirt shop into a complete full service promotional branding company that helps clients market and promote their businesses using the direct response marketing strategies that we've learned from the real-deal marketing gurus like Dan Kennedy and Bill Glazer and combined it with the power of promotional products.

As self-diagnosed marketing junkies, we've developed this unique approach to creating outrageously effective marketing by combing the power of the $20 billion dollar promotional products industry along with the explosive time tested strategies of direct response marketing.

We are the originators of this powerful combination that creates explosive results for our clients. We don't claim to be some kind of marketing guru. We simply discovered the lethal combination of direct response marketing and the power of promotional products.

Throughout our 15 years in marketing, we've helped entrepreneurs, marketers and businesses of all sizes create outrageous promotions that are outrageously successful. To get more info on how we can help you easily & quickly flood you business with more prospects, clients and sales than you can handle please give us a call at 305-888-7301 or visit us at www.outrageouspromotions.com

Contents

Chapter One……………………….. 23

Chapter Two…………………….. 29

Chapter Three………………….... 37

Chapter Four……………………… 43

Chapter Five…………………….. 47

Chapter Six……………………… 53

Chapter Seven……………………. 59

Chapter Eight……………………. 65

Chapter Nine……………………. 69

Chapter Ten……………………... 77

Chapter Eleven………………….. 83

Section Two……………………. 91

> "Discover The Top Secret Weapons That Some Small to Mid-Sized Companies Have Used to Beat The Pants Off Their Competitors As Well As The Big Fortune 500 Companies; While Creating A Whopping 4,000% Return On Investment, Generating $528,000 In New Orders, Increasing Revenues By 38% In A Single Quarter and Driving Over 3,200 People to A Website, While Working Less and Not Hiring An Expensive "Marketing Guru" Or An Over Priced Advertising Agency"

If you own a business of any kind: How would you like to stop being an "Advertising and Marketing Victim" and Once and for all Stop Wasting Money on Worthless Advertising?

Would you want to once and for all get accurately measurable, quick results from each and every dollar you put into ANY kind of advertising, marketing and promotions?

Would You Like To Stop Wasting Time On Cold Call Prospecting Grunt Work?

If you answered YES! To any or all of these question…Excellent. Then you are ready to instantly soar to the next level of success and income in your business.

If you're ready then do yourself a favor and take the time to read this book because you'll discover these incredible, proven, top secret weapons that will cause a virtual <u>avalanche</u> of new business for you in the following days, weeks, and months.

This book will transform your business.

Now's The Time!

To Instantly Begin...

Now's The Time To Flood Your Business with More New Clients, Prospects, And Sales than You Can Handle!

Let me start by saying that you've made an incredibly smart decision to starting reading this book. Few people are wise enough to understand what it takes to truly make it in the highly competitive business world.

You're the exception... you're probably a leading edge thinker, an outside the box kind of person and it's probably safe to say that you are more aware than any of your friends and business peers about what it requires to truly become a successful business person in this day and age.

You're proud to be a business owner. Owning a business is part of the American dream. You've worked hard to have the freedom that comes with owning a business and you're delighted to be currently living the American dream.

Your hard work has paid off but in order to continue living the dream you must find the time to give your business the special attention it wants, needs, and deserves.

The Small Business Administration states the following statistics:
- 590,000 new businesses are added to the already existing 3.5 million U.S. small businesses every year.
- 50% of those new businesses will fail within the first year.
- Another 45% will not make it past the fifth year.

So why Do 95% of All Small Businesses Eventually Fail?

Outrageous Promotions That Are Outrageously Effective

Every year small businesses fail because they didn't pay enough attention to marketing and promoting their business. When asked why some of the top reasons given were…

- *I just didn't have enough time to get to the marketing and promotions.*
- *I couldn't come up with good ideas to market and promote my business.*
- *I didn't understand the difference between marketing and selling.*
- *I thought I couldn't afford to market and promote my business.*

And you might be thinking that you're not like those businesses. You've worked hard and business is doing better and better every year because of your hard work and dedication.

But you also realize that as the business continues to grow it is getting harder and harder to find the time to come up with the next great marketing idea.

Like most, you are always busy. Having to stay on top of everything and everyone gets time consuming. Who has the time or energy to even think about marketing and promotions?

But you gotta admit it's been way too long and without cutting into family time, working weekends or hiring an expensive marketing guru or an overpriced Ad agency it's going to be even longer before the next great marketing idea comes along.

Let's face it, you have way too much on your plate already and the last thing you need is another one of those high priced "marketing gurus" who can't seem to run a profitable business themselves telling you how to improve your business.

I'm not here to tell you how to run your business nor am I one of those high priced "marketing gurus".

I simply want to show you how some small, mid sized and even large businesses have come across the tools to transform their marketing to create it into a finely tuned, highly effective revenue generating, money making marketing machines.

Let me also point out that it doesn't matter if you own a company selling sophisticated software to the Fortune 500 or a local ice cream shop, incredibly what you're about to discover in this book can "re-invent" your entire marketing process for the better!

Before you continue to invest your time reading this book, let me ask you a few more questions to help determine if you even need to bother reading the rest of this book.

1. Would you like to cut out all the waste from your company's marketing and make your sales people immensely more productive?
2. Would you like to posses new, powerful ways to attract prospects that are pre-disposed to buy from you?
3. Would you like to end cold calling and have prospects CALLING YOU to set up appointments?
4. Would you like to have highly qualified prospects eager to do business with you?

If you answered NO to all of the above questions, then please don't waste another minute of your time, reading this book.

However if you answered YES to any of the questions, you should continue reading every word because on the following pages you're going to discover…

The easy to use tools that will allow you to:
- ATTRACT… a flood of new customers at will
- CREATE… instant cash flow surges in your business
- DOMINATE… any target market you choose

And that's just for starters!

Not only will you start making more money, but you'll have more time do the things you really want to do…like go hit the golf course, spend time with the family or go on a much needed vacation or whatever.

The point is that when you have the right marketing tools in place the money keeps rolling in!

It's important to note, I said having the right "marketing tools" not "sales tools"

Because Success Is ALL About Marketing, Not About Sales.

What's the difference between marketing and selling? That's a great question, I'm glad you asked.

Marketing is about attracting prospects to your business that are ready to buy as opposed to chasing after prospects to sell them.

Prospects LOVE to buy but they HATE to be sold.

(Please pay close attention because you're about to get a crash course in effective marketing, forget what you learned in college.)

First you must understand that every business is also in the marketing business.

Let me repeat that…No matter what business you're in, no matter what product you sell or what service you provide, you're not only in that business but you're also in the business of marketing the product or service of that business.

Allow me to explain…If you're an Accountant, you are in the accounting business and also in the business of marketing your accounting firm.

Or if you own an ice cream shop, you're in the ice cream business and you're also in the business of marketing your ice cream shop

Do you see my point?

Let me give you another example of what I mean…

It doesn't matter if you're a good accountant, doctor, plumber, printer, or whatever because if you fail as a marketer it's hard to get clients.

And without clients, you're out of business. QUICK!

Let me give you two scenarios:

1. You're a GOOD marketer but a Bad accountant
2. You're a GOOD accountant but a Bad marketer

I don't know about you but I'd prefer to be in the first scenario.

Remember what I mentioned earlier? Marketing is about attracting people to your business. So if you're able to attract clients then you simply hire a good accountant to work for you.

The better you learn to market your business, the better your business will do and the more accountants you will hire.

So what's my point? Well let me assure you that my point is not to encourage you to be a bad accountant.

The point I'm trying to get across to you is that you're a marketer first and everything else second.

Nothing should come before marketing your business.

The businesses that fully understand this are the ones that are part of the TOP 5% of businesses that succeed. The TOP 5% get the fact that marketing must come before selling.

MARKETING ALWAYS COMES FIRST, Selling always comes second.

Forget the old saying "Nothing happens until you sell something"

I'm here to tell you "Nothing sells until you market something"

Marketing is easy, selling is hard.

Remember… people LOVE to buy but they HATE to be sold.

I'll use an example to prove my point…

It may take me a day or two to create a direct mail marketing campaign. The investment of time will allow me to mail hundreds even thousands of prospects at one time.

On the other hand, instead I could've spent day in and day out enduring the constant rejection of cold calling to unqualified prospects to have only reached a couple of people at the end of every day.

Miserable and filled with rejection I'd have to find the courage and the will to do it again and again as the weeks progress before I close just one lousy deal.

But with a marketing campaign in less than 48 hours I'm able to reach numerous businesses at the same time. So that those who are interested can raise their hands above the crowd, reach to the phone and contact me.

See? Marketing is so much easier than sales!

Well If Marketing Is So Easy… Why Does Almost No One Use It?

Another great question!

The fact is that marketing is easy only when you know how to use it. You can spend yourself broke trying to figure out on your own how to market your business effectively.

You'll go broke even faster if you listen to "Big Media" sales reps. Do what the BIG COMPANIES do is the mindset.

It probably goes something like this…

"They make millions… they know what they're doing, if it works for them it'll work for you"

Six months down the road, by the time you realize that you've spent BIG MONEY on BIG MEDIA marketing campaigns that produced small results if any, you're deep in debt and desperate for a solution.

So… if BIG MEDIA is not the solution to your problems. What is?

The solution came to me when I took over an almost bankrupt business back in 2000.

You won't believe that the solution could be this simple… still… it is!

Since I know you might have some doubts about this simple solution that I'm about to reveal to you… so I'm prepared to prove it to you.

You'll read later on, directly from other business owners, how shockingly amazed they are at the BIG RESULTS they're producing.

Your fellow business owners resolved your same marketing problems through…The Power of Promotional Products

That's Right…The Best Marketing Tool for Your Business is the Power of Promotional Products!

Promotional Products DO Work!

Actually, they work like crazy.

My clients have experienced first hand the power of promotional products…or as I like to say promotional products that work. And once they saw how great our marketing strategies and campaigns worked when applied to promo products, they were hooked.

They started with something as simple and inexpensive as a promotional product and continued building from there as they gained the knowledge and the right tools to succeed!

But I still have to prove it to you.

You won't believe the BIG RESULTS that these business; small and large, have created using the power of promotional products to create outrageous promotions that are outrageously effective and successful.

I've kept the some of the names confidential in order to protect their ideas from their competition. But names are irrelevant because the proof as they say is in the pudding…

"Your promotional products that work concept is GREAT! After reading your report I had the idea for the Martini Shaker with the tag line shaking things up with our guarantee and that has resulted in my business experiencing a fourth quarter increase of 38% over last year. I couldn't have achieved such dramatic results without your concept." Nancy, Pino & Associates, Fl

"Dear Rob, my son and I together came up with a marketing campaign using your concepts. The planning guide you sent about using promotional products to compliment our marketing was the reason for the idea. We used our name Empire Plumbing to build a theme. We ordered a travel size chess game to give to prospects and customers. The chess set was such a BIG HIT. The theme was a natural fit with our name so we are now using chess pieces and a checkerboard background on our brochures as well. Next thing we're working on is an idea for our new "Checkmate Offer" & "King of all Guarantees." Anthony Montalvo, Owner Empire Plumbing

Outrageous Promotions That Are Outrageously Effective

"I'm the Marketing Director at a car dealership. My boss is obsessed with "Going Green" so much so that he asked me to develop a marketing strategy to sell more hybrid models. I heard from a friend about your strategies of using promotional items as part of the marketing campaign. Since proper tire inflation is essential to fuel conservation I went with a gift set that consisted of a tire gauge, mini flashlight and a pen. The whole thing was presented in a sleek case that fit perfectly in the glove compartment. We ran a newspaper ad that featured the free gift with the test drive of a hybrid model. The results were spectacular. My boss thought the turnout was amazing and I looked brilliant." Max Medina

"We kicked off an internal sales contest using a series of promotional items that employees could earn depending on their sales volume. We included Swiss Army Knives, embroidered golf shirts, leather jackets and digital cameras. It has become almost bragging rights for the sales staff. The sales contest using your ideas brought in a $2.2 million sales increase, exceeding the original goal by $700,000. I can honestly say that it was all due to incorporating promo products as a key part of the sales contest."
Rene Garcia; Action Manufacturing in Texas

"My sales team & I conduct a sales blitz about once a month, where we stop in to see potential new clients and drop off our promo packages. Last month we ordered insulated cooler bags with our logo and put in a branded bottle of water and a branded bag of un-popped popcorn. Now we have a reason to "POP IN" and introduce ourselves and leave an afternoon snack. We then follow up with the contact to ask for an appointment for an afternoon snack. Using the afternoon snack has increased our appointment ratio by 58%. I think the casual message of meeting over an afternoon snack appeals to prospects more than a lengthy lunch or a sales appointment. My sales team and I would like to thank you for showing us that marketing comes before selling." Patricia Acevedo, Staffing Plus

"After reading your letter I quickly incorporated a referral promotion using the power of promo products. Whenever I send clients an invoice, I slip in a referral request along with a photo of the referral gift. I'm currently using a pair of crystal candle holders even the men like it I think they give it to their wives. It's a great incentive that has produced multiple referrals from clients. I plan on changing the item every few months to keep them excited about always referring new clients. The investment is well worth it and a lot more cost-effective than I thought. I've already made my investment back by landing several new clients." Ana Fernandez, Event Planner, Coral Gables Florida

"Your outrageous promotions concept has taught us a way to set ourselves apart from everybody else. We used a branded poker chip with a "Don't Gamble with your financial future". The promotion was designed to drive traffic to our website by offering a FREE REPORT "Don't Gamble With Your Financial Future…" We sent out 1,800 pieces and got 3,200 hits on our website. Yes, we got more than we sent out; I'm still amazed by the results. Scott Dorado, Financial Publishing

"For my Bait & Tackle Shop I was looking for a way to promote the annual fishing contest. After reading your letter, I decided to try using a free sign up gift. I wasn't sure how well it would work but I guess it did well because I got 12 more contestants than last year. I can't wait till next year to find a promo gift that will bring in even more contestants" TJ from TJ's Bait Shack

"As a distributor of Latin foods and spices it can some times be tough to get the grocery stores to take up shelf space for a new product. With what I've learned from the promotional products that work concept I came up with an incentive for my customers. I told them that if they bought 3 cases of the new Latin Chicken Soup line I would give them free soup mugs. This worked out good for them and me. The grocery store would give a free mug with the purchase of every 3 cans of soup creating goodwill with their customers. The free mug with purchase also meant more sales for them and me. And of course, the mug was branded with the product logo. Double Whammy." Hola Foods, GA

"The hospital I work for was experiencing difficulty with the news media using the proper name of our newest out reach center in their news stories. Someone in marketing had read your report about the power of promotional products and we reached out to your company for help. We selected a pill bottle filled with paper clips and a prescription label printed with the name of our outreach center. We were stressed out about the concept but the reporters thought it was a fun and clever way to set the record straight. I saw the container on one reporter's desk several months later." Nancy Tucker, Public Relations

"The catering business relies heavily on building relationship with event and wedding planners. I needed a way to get their attention so that I could schedule them for a private tasting. After hearing you speak a recent conference, I was able to come up with a hot sauce bottle with the invite printed right on the label. Now every time I send out an invitation I always get an RSVP. Works like a charm, I love it. PROMOTIONAL PRODUCTS ROCK" Tracy Sherman, Edible Memories, Las Vegas

"My wife and I have owned and operated a Bed & Breakfast going on 7 years next month. After coming across your info, we started thinking of a way to use the power of promotional products to increase our reservation rate. Knowing that women tend to make the choice of which bed & breakfast to book we thought a manicure set would work nicely. We experienced an increase of about 30% on reservation by just adding the gift. And by the way we love how our logo looks, thank you." Joey & Sarah, Proud Owners!

"When we added a car wash to our chain of quick lube service centers we were not getting as much traffic as we thought we would. We used the promotional products that work idea to help get the word out. We choose a large chip clip with the car wash info on one side and on the other side the name of the quick lube service center. We then clipped two coupons for the car wash. One was for them to keep and use. The other was for them to pass on to a friend. With in just a couple of days the number of car washes more than doubled at all 3 locations"
Nick Babulus, Express Lube, Norfolk VA

"We tried sending out inexpensive promotional products before but everybody does that. After taking the time to read your report we took your advice and instead of giving away cheap stuff to everybody and not standing out. We invested the same amount of money but targeted fewer prospects. This allowed us to spend more per prospect and make it spectacular. The plan was to target our 15 largest prospects using the theme "Industrial Strength" and we used a series of steel promotional products. We used a steel CD case, a portfolio and a business card case filled with our business cards to perfectly tie in to the tag line. The reaction was immediate and overwhelming. More than half of the 15 prospects contacted us, which has led to six meetings, 12 requests for quotes and a total of $78,274.00 in sales. Not bad for a $2,025 investment. We were expecting to just get our foot in the door, but we ended up getting some great business. We will definitely come up with another outrageous promotion very soon."

"Rob using your strategies we had an extremely successful marketing campaign for the opening of our new branch office. The promotion

was targeted to clients, prospects, media, and industry associations. We received an incredible amount of feedback and calls from the campaign. As of today, we have generated $380,000 of new business for the firm. This campaign was much more effective than running an ad and sending out a press release."
Lee, Lux Design

Have I proved my case?

I think we can both agree these businesses are achieving

BIG RESULTS!

Do you see how this promotional products that work concept is creating OUTRAGEOUS RESULTS and changing many people's businesses?

And it will change your business too.

> **"A Well-Thought-Out Promotional Products Marketing Campaign Is One of the Most Powerful Yet Cost-Effective Marketing Tools That Any Business Can Use To Boost Results Almost Overnight."**

Obviously, this powerful new concept of using the power of promo products has nothing in common with the traditional ways of using promotional products.

But really, who says that promotional products should only be used to hand out contact information?

Who says that promotional products should be boring and used the same way as every other business around?

Just like I said, the solution is simple... *Promotional Products* needs to become a key player in your marketing game plan.

There are the two main reasons why this is the solution to your marketing problems:

1. When I talk about the power of promotional products, I am not talking about the traditional giveaways, trinkets or swag...No I am talking about **Promotional Products that Work**. They deliver OUTRAGEOUS RESULTS.

In this book, you're going to discover how to get the most from this powerful-targeted media. You'll no longer view branded promotional products as simply handouts or giveaways but rather as a cost effective method for tracking results and getting your marketing message in front of exactly the people who need to see it and do that on a repetitive basis.

2. Unlike other media, promotional products continue to work because they serve as a reminder that remains long after creating "Residual Marketing" for your business for many years to come. In addition, they create positive feelings about your company.

Promo Products are tangible, memorable and reinforce your message.

Using the *Power of Promotional Products That Work is* an incredibly effective way to promote your business simply because unlike other media that is quickly discarded, your brand is constantly in front of your prospects and/or customers until the time comes that they're ready to do business with you.

This powerful new breed of promotional products has several key strengths…

- **Target Ability**: Unlike other media your message is delivered to those you target
- **Exposure Frequency**: Items get in front and remain in front of your target
- **Creative Impact**: The creative possibilities of promotional products are endless
- **Goodwill**: The only advertising with a built-in "Thank You"
- **Flexibility:** When properly chosen they can be used in virtually any situation
- **Motivation**: Promotional products can motivate your target to take action

Promo Products That Work can support a wide array of objectives that include:

- Promoting awareness for new products and/or services
- Reinforcing existing products and/or services
- Improving existing Lead Generation efforts by getting more new prospects to contact you
- Increasing trade show booth traffic and trade show sales
- Recognizing and Retaining existing customers
- Reactivating old accounts
- Motivating sales staff and promoting sales contest
- Rewarding & Recognizing employee performance and workplace safety

Do you see how important it is for you to make *Promotional Products That Work* part of your marketing mix today?

This is the beginning to a completely new approach to your marketing and sales.

You're going to discover The Power of *Promo Products That Work*... PLUS the knowledge to make the most out of them.

You see, I've learned that the right tools without knowledge are useless.

But knowledge, without the right tools to take action, is meaningless.

I'll personally provide you with **the knowledge and training to make the most out of both!**

This combination of knowledge along with great marketing tools like *Promotional Products That Work* will transform your business and lead you to the Top 5%.

And isn't transforming your business and becoming part of that Top 5%, the whole point of why you're reading this book.

The knowledge that leads to higher sales is...

The lethal combination of the *Power of Promo Products that Work* together with the most explosive direct-response marketing secrets.

These are the marketing secrets that I've discovered from the REAL DEAL Marketing Gurus like Dan Kennedy & Bill Glazer.
As a matter of fact here's a picture of me with Dan Kennedy at the GKIC Marketing Super Conference.

Outrageous Promotions That Are Outrageously Effective

These guys know what they are talking about and they walk the talk.

I invest thousands of dollars per year and 100's of hours learning, reading and studying their strategies to find the most highly effective ways to use those top direct-response marketing strategies to work with the powerful new breed of *Promo Products That Work* to gain OUTRAGEOUS RESULTS.

Imagine what it'll do for your business to discover these direct-response marketing strategies that you can combine with the power of *Promotional Products That Work* to instantly transform your business.

Are you ready to transform your marketing?

Are you ready to change the way you do business FOREVER?

Are you ready for OUTRAGEOUS RESULTS?

Then Let The Transformation Begin!!!

The Power of Promotional Products That Work is transforming all kinds of businesses.

I guarantee you that once you discover how *easy and profitable* it is to boost sales with these simple yet powerful strategies, you'll start to grow your business at a more rapid pace than you've ever seen before.

Doesn't it feel great to *FINALLY* discover the knowledge and the tools to easily and automatically boost sales?

And what will this mean for your business? **How will you feel about…?**

- ATTRACTING… a flood of new customers at will
- CREATING… instant cash flow surges in your business
- DOMINATING… any target market you choose

It's been a long time since *you've felt this good about your marketing*, hasn't it?

Well, I have EVEN MORE GOOD NEWS FOR YOU…

How would you feel if I told you that not only will you boost your sales but you will also…

Save Money and Generate a Positive Return On Your Investment!

How much more would you invest for marketing that delivers the kind of results as the stories you've just read about?

15% more? 30%? Even 50% more?

Basically, it doesn't matter, does it?

Who cares if you have to pay $50, $100 even $200 more when the power of *Promotional Products That Work* can be responsible **for doubling and even tripling sales**?

So… what would you say if I told you that you will not pay more for using *Promo Products that Work*?

What? No, it's not impossible. On the contrary, you'll pay less than what you're currently paying for other advertising media.

The Power of Promo Products That Work concept will actually bring in more revenue than any other media… So it basically cost you nothing to use them as they more than pay for themselves.

Because unlike traditional promotional products or big media marketing, the *Power of Promo Products That Work* will generate a positive Return On Investment (ROI), so in actuality you pay less than traditional promotional products that produce no results and instead drain your budget and cause you to miss the sale.

Are You Ready to Get Started with Promo Products that Work?

Everyday you wait to "think about it" or "get around to" is costing you money in missed sales…money that could be in your bank account.

The Time to Take Action Is… Now!

I want you to read all the way thru this book with an open mind.

Then go to the Outrageous Promotions Swipe File section.

This section will provide you with ideas for planning campaigns, creating your theme, choosing your target and defining your objective.

I know you're excited to get started but remember that I first recommend that you go thru the entire book.

Pay close attention as you read the sections proving the power of promotional products. The results of these studies can be eye opening and incredibly insightful.

As you go thru the results think of how you can achieve the same results for your marketing using the power of promotional products.

When you get in to the outrageous promotions swipe file section do not just read the ones that you think apply to your business. I advise that you go thru all of them because it will help you come up with ideas and marketing strategies that you may not have thought of.

I guarantee that you will come up with ways of using promotional products that you wouldn't of thought of had you not taken the time to read this book.

<u>Alright I can feel the excitement so lets get on to the nitty gritty.</u>

Chapter One

Discover the Power of Promotional Products

I do not know about you but when I think about Promotional Products… I cannot think of any other advertising medium that is victim to so much misunderstanding, misuse and miseducation as promotional products.

Even though, it is one of the fastest growing, most effective forms of advertising being utilized today. And the only reason this $20 billion dollar a year industry continues to grow is because promotional products DO WORK!

In this book, I'm going to show you how to make them work for you.

I'm going to show you how to create outrageously effective promotions using the power of promo products.

The popularity of promotional products continues to grow and in recent years, more and more companies have discovered the marketing power of promotional products.

The Promotional Products Association International (PPAI) surveyed business people about promotional products. When they asked respondents if they've used promotional products to promote their business an astonishing 95% said yes.

Promotional products as a marketing tool has been used for well over a 100 years. Did you know the earliest use of promotional products tracks all the way back to George Washington who used printed buttons as part of his political campaign.

However, they did not become known as promotional products the way you and I know them, until 1870 when a burlap schoolbook bag was used to promote a business.

Today the most successful companies know that promotional products are no longer seen as just simple give-a-ways or handouts. Promotional products have evolved into a very effective and powerful marketing tool.

The reason they are so powerful comes from their ability to get an effective, targeted message in front of exactly the leads and clients you need to reach and keep your message there until the time comes that they're ready to do business with you.

Promotional products are by far the most cost-effective way to reach and to motivate your target audience.

First of all, they get your marketing message in front of your audience and second and most important they remain in front of them as a constant reminder until the decision is made to do business with your company.

Let me give you a great example of how powerful promotional products can be.

An article in the Wall Street Journal mentioned that the recipient may see an imprinted coffee mug as often as 25 times a day.

So let me ask you this…Could you afford to reach a prospect 25 times a day using TV, Radio or Newspaper every single day until they make that buying decision?

I didn't think so. I mean unless you're Coke or Nike most companies really do not have that kind of money to burn.

However, the constant exposure to your message doesn't stop with just your prospect because everyone that comes into contact with the recipient of that mug is also exposed to your marketing message.

As you can see, promotional products generate multiple impressions and are constantly increasing your brand awareness, which is one of the keys to increasing market share.

And increased market share equals increased revenue.

Just take a moment to look around your home or office and you're bound to find an imprinted pen, mug, mouse pad, calendar or some other items imprinted with a company logo. And the reason is because they want you to remember their name, product or service when it's time to buy.

Promotional products are everywhere and with over 750,000 promotional products available to help get your message in front of your target market it makes it a whole lot easier when you know which ones are the most popular items. According to PPAI, the top 10 product categories are...

1) Wearable's including t-shirts, polo shirts, button downs, jackets and caps
2) Writing instrument pens, pencils highlighters etc
3) Desk/office/business accessories folders, desk set, calculators, memo pads, post it notes, note cubes, desk clock, etc
4) Calendars wall and wallet, desk & pocket as well as planners and day timers

5) Drink ware includes all glass, ceramic, plastic and stainless steel mugs, tumblers, and water bottles
6) Bags including tote bags, shopping bags, gift bags, duffel bags, laptop bags and briefcases
7) Personal products such as key tags, pocket knives, grooming aids, lighters, sunglasses, lip balm ,umbrellas, biz card holders, etc
8) Computer accessories mouse pads, monitor frames, wrist pads, USB ports, flash drives
9) Kitchen products and House wares like candles, picture frames, flashlights, first aid kits, tool kits, etc
10) Sporting/leisure and travel, golf accessories, binoculars, sunscreen, picnic products, etc

It also helps you to know that they can be used to achieve a variety of marketing objectives. PPAI reports that the top twelve ways promotional products are used is…

1) Business gifts to foster customer goodwill and loyalty in order to increase customer retention
2) Stimulating tradeshow booth traffic with pre-show promotions and post-show follow up
3) Generating sales leads and set appointments
4) Creating brand awareness of new products and/or services as well as increasing the overall brand awareness
5) Increasing direct mail response rates
6) Increasing retail store traffic
7) Promoting a sales contest
8) Motivating and rewarding dealers and distributors
9) Improving, rewarding and recognizing employee performance
10) Stimulating more referrals
11) Enhancing a company's image in the public eye
12) Promoting employee safety programs

In preparing to write this book, I asked a number of my clients why and how they use promotional products and some of the answers given to me were…

"Brand reminders and sales increase"

"More name recognition which equals more volume"

"Keeping us top of mind, for a person to think about us first"

"I want to create a positive impression of my business"

"To generate word of mouth and referrals"

"Building business relationships between us and our customers and prospects"

"If sales reps give out gifts then the sales reps are more likely to get an appointment or make the sale"

"Customer loyalty is a big thing. Putting my name in front of people and getting the word of mouth that comes from someone seeing the promotional product"

"Increasing traffic to our tradeshow booth"

"I get better response to my mailing if I send an item or offer an item"

Before we move on to chapter two let me give you a few brief examples of simple promotions that focused on using the power of promotional products.

I'll get into more detailed case studies later into his book but I just want to give you some quick examples.

- A fitness club promoted its cookbook to members with a free healthy eating pocket slide chart that showed people how they can keep cholesterol levels low by choosing foods with good fats.

- A fire department used a bandage dispenser as a giveaway at an open house for a new fire station. They printed the fire departments logo, new address and fire safety phone numbers.

- A local bank used a branded "Summer Relief Kit" as an incentive for people to open a savings account in the slow summer months. They featured their logo and a summer savings tagline.

- A pharmaceutical company distributed a skin cancer chart thru physician's offices; the product showed patients how to examine their skin for moles that might be cancerous.

- A veterinary clinic gave branded pet food bag clips with a built in scoop to new clients. The clips were so popular they started offering them for sale in the lobby area.

Chapter Two

The Strength of Promotional Products

Many people even those who consider themselves truly sophisticated marketers completely fail to understand how to effectively harness the power of promotional products as a marketing tool.

Until they read this book.

Those who talk about handouts, giveaways and "Logo'ed Stuff" have completely overlooked the key applications and opportunities that could improve their marketing results and increase their bottom line.

Giveaways and handouts are not where the power of promotional products lies.

The power is in creating a promotional marketing campaign that will allow you to know without a doubt what's working in your marketing and what's not.

Let me give you an example of the wrong way and the right way to use promotional products.

First, let me show you the wrong way. Let's say that a car dealership orders 1,000 key chains printed with their logo as a giveaway to 1,000 people within a 10-mile radius of the dealership.

After giving away the 1,000 key chains, the dealership would have no way of knowing what the results were. They would end up thinking that the promotional product giveaway simply did not work.

Now let me show you what a car dealership that read this book would do instead. The right way to do it is to create a promotional products that work marketing campaign instead of just a giveaway.

The first thing to do is to think about the goal of the campaign.

The dealer wants to 1) create some awareness 2) encourage people to come in for a test drive and 3) sell some cars.

Based on these objectives the dealer will send out the same 1,000 key chains to the same 1,000 people within a 10 mile radius but this time they'll attach a key to the key chain and let people know that if they come in and try the key on a car inside the showroom they could win a prize.

If the key opens the door, they get a prize. The prize could be a travel mug or electronic tire gauge.

They could also let people know that anyone who comes in and takes a test drive will get their choice of free gift such as a visor organizer or trunk organizer.

In addition, anyone who buys a car gets their choice of a free roadside emergency kit or a pair of stainless steel travel mugs.

Let me take a moment here to give you a strategy that I learned from Dan Kennedy and Bill Glazer.

When it comes to using a free gift as an incentive always, I repeat always, give them a choice of gifts. Because in the prospects mind first it becomes about which gift they want.

Once they've decided which gift they want then they will start to rationalize the buying decision because they have chosen a gift that they really want. This is a very powerful strategy that will motivate the buying decision.

Okay so back to our car dealership. Now they have a promotion instead of a giveaway. At the end of the promotion, the dealership can say we sent out 1,000 key chains and 62 people came in to try their key and win a free prize.

23 people ended up taking a test drive and 7 bought a car. The average sale was $21,000 so the promotion generated a $147,000 in sales.

Now that's a powerful promotion… that beats a giveaway any day.

That my friend is the right way to use the power of promotional products to create an outrageously effective marketing campaign.

Most businesses don't realize that just giving away promotional products doesn't work because there is no real reason for it to work.

There was no objective to the promotion.

Again, there is a huge difference between a promotion and a giveaway.

Now don't get me wrong there is a time and place for using giveaways. If you want to drive traffic to a tradeshow booth, or create brand awareness and brand exposure or want to thank your clients for a purchase then a giveaway works great.

However, if you want to attract attention, motivate your prospect to take action and buy your product and/or service then you will need a promotion rather than just a basic giveaway.

In this book, you'll discover how to finally create accurate, measurable and effective marketing campaigns using the power of promotional products that work.

You'll discover the key factors for creating outrageously powerful promotions and get some good solid action oriented advice on how to use the power of promotional marketing for the benefit of your company.

First, you need to truly understand the power of promotional products.

So let's go over some of the key strengths.

Here are 15 very good reasons why promotional products are so effective virus any and all other media.

1) Target ability: Unlike any other media with promo products your marketing message is delivered only to those you target therefore eliminating the waste associated with other media. Mass media tends to be a shotgun approach but with promotional products, you can target as few as 1 or as many as 100, 1,000 or 10,000.

2) They are tangible: Promotional products are memorable because they become a tangible reminder of your company.

3) They inform: The real purpose of a promotional product is to inform the target about your company's products and/or service.

4) They remind: Once the target becomes informed, the promotional products continue to work as a constant reminder of your products and/or service until the buying decision is made.

5) They motivate: Although the target is aware and reminded of your products and/or service, they may need an extra nudge to actually make a purchase. A well chosen promotional product can motivate your target to take action.

6) They Support: The current buzzword in marketing is IMC (Integrated Marketing Communication) IMC refers to having marketing pieces that all compliment each other. Integrating promotional products with other campaigns such as radio ads, TV ads and direct mail will help you measure the results and get a better return on investment.

7) Longevity: One of the greatest advantages of promotional products over other media such as TV or radio is their ability to make and leave a long lasting impression on the recipient. Unlike other media, promotional products tend to stay around and be seen again and again. While your newspaper ad becomes birdcage liner, a coffee mug, mouse pad or calendar will occupy a visible spot in an office or home for many years to come.

8) Measurability: When used properly promotional products can be used to measure the success of a marketing campaign. You can easily track your response rate just like the car dealership did. Another good example of this is a company that worked with us to motivate customers and prospects to visit its booth at a tradeshow. They sent out to 1,000 invitations and included a nice card with a slot for a pen – but the pen wasn't

included. The recipient was asked to stop by the booth to receive their free pen. The company ordered enough pens for 400 people, which would be well over the standard 1 to 2% response rate. After the show the company had to order an additional 320 pens to met the final response rate of 72%

9) High return on investment: Because promotional products are so targeted, they generate a much higher return on investment than other media.

10) Built in thank you: It's the only form of advertising that someone will actually thank you for, when was the last time someone thanked you for running an ad in the local newspaper…other than the newspaper sales rep.

11) Involvement: promotional products can involve all five senses: touch, sight, sound, smell and taste. The involvement of all five senses creates a memory hook that makes the recall of the marketing message much higher.

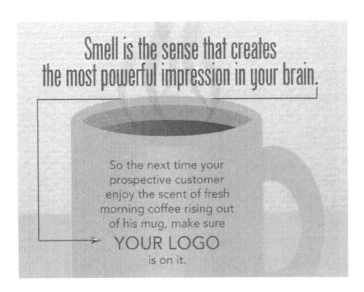

12) Social proof: When someone uses a promotional product, it indicates that the person has a favorable working relationship with that company which implies they endorse it therefore creating social proof to others about your company.

13) Customer goodwill: When used correctly to show appreciation it creates goodwill with the recipients every time they look at or use the promotional products. According to research done by Baylor University, promotional products favorably improve customers attitudes toward a company and their representatives. By using promotional products, companies significantly enhance customer loyalty and improve goodwill over competitors.

14) Creative flexibility: The creative possibilities with promotional products are endless. When properly chosen and with the right message imprinted they can be used in virtually any marketing situation.

15) Usefulness: Who isn't always looking for a pen or doesn't use a coffee mug. Who wouldn't appreciate receiving a tote bag while attending a tradeshow? Or a gym bag to gather sneakers and balls for the kid's soccer practice. One of the biggest reasons promotional products are powerful is because they're items people keep and use on a daily basis.

It's no wonder that according to a new study from the Advertising Specialty Institute (ASI) promotional products beat nearly all other types of marketing and advertising media including, TV, radio and print when it comes to cost per impression (CPI)

The ASI study shows that an astronomical 84% of the people that receive a promotional product remember the name of the advertiser on the promotional product up to one year later.

Want more hard evidence that promotional products work. In the next chapter, we will cover 10 reasons why you should start using the power of promotional products in ALL of your marketing and advertising campaigns.

Chapter Three:

Hard Evidence of the Power of Promotional Products

In this chapter, I'm going to give you hard evidence proving the power of promotional products.

The Advertising Specialty Institute® (ASI) released a new study revealing that promotional products (also known as advertising specialties) beat TV, radio, and print advertising mediums for attracting new customers and better lead generation. So let me start with…

1) **They'll remember your business**
   Do you really think that a typical consumer can remember the advertiser on a TV commercial they saw last night? How about an ad from reading the morning newspaper? I wouldn't bet on it.

   But they're 84% more likely to recall the advertiser on a promotional product they received up to 12 months ago.

   The study shows that number goes up to 93% of those who received logoed apparel such as T-shirts, caps and jackets. Remember wearables are the most popular promo products.

2) **They'll have a better impression of your business**
   42% of people who receive your promotional product will have a more favorable impression of your business after receiving the promo product.

That's right almost half of the people who receive a promo product will think more favorably of the business that gave it to them. Again, the number can be even higher for certain products such as bags, t-shirts and caps.

Add promotional products to your next marketing campaign and you can be sure your prospects and clients will see you in a more favorable light than all the others.

3) **They'll do more business with you**
How sure can you be that when you send a prospect or client a promotional product that they'll actually do business with you?

Pretty darn sure because according to the ASI Study 62% of people have done business with the advertiser after receiving a promotional product from that business.

Therefore, by sending them a promo product you're doing one of two things, you're either motivating a prospect to become a customer and/or enhancing a current customer to order.

4) **Your message remains until they are ready to do business with you.**
Think your client threw away that mug you sent him last week? That's highly doubtful because according to the new research most people keep promotional products an average of 10 months and may keep an item with a high-perceived value for even longer.

Think about how often a prospect or client will see that mug, pen or calendar…That equals a lot of brand exposure for your company for pennies on the dollar. Try doing that with other media.

5) **People keep items that are useful.**
If you're trying to find the right promotional product for your next marketing campaign consider the fact that people tend to keep items that are useful.

Items like pens, mugs and bags are kept for a long time because your prospects and clients will use them over and over again. So pick a product that's useful and it will give your brand more staying power.

6) **Promotional products are frequently used.**
If somebody tells you that nobody will use the bag you gave away at your last tradeshow do not believe a word they're saying.

The research shows that items such as bags and apparel are the most frequently used in the promotional products world.

On average, a business-person will use the same bag more than nine times per month. Just think of all the exposure your brand gets as that bag with your logo is toted around.

7) **Many promotional products are used as often as daily.**
Bags and apparel aren't the only items that get major exposure. Some promotional products like pens, mugs, mouse pads, calendars, note pads, etc are used multiple times per day.

If you're looking to have your brand in front of a prospect or client everyday, promo products can do just that and without breaking the bank.

8) **Higher number of impressions.**

    If you're measuring the Return On Investment (ROI) of your marketing efforts (and you should be) it's important for you to know that a single promotional product can deliver several hundred even thousands of impressions per month.

    For instance, a single logoed bag averages 1,038 impressions per month according to the new study. If you gave out 1,000 branded bags to prospects and clients that would create an astronomical 1,038,000 impressions per month.

    And the best part is you get the additional exposure at no additional cost to you.

9) **Cost-Per-Impressions (CPI) is fractions of a penny.**

    If your marketing dollars are tight consider the fact that the average cost per impression of a promotional product is $0.004 (Yes, there are two zeros before the four…it's not a misprint).

That's a fraction of a cent per impression and that number is even smaller for certain products like calendars, T-shirts and caps.

Let me quickly share with you some of the other findings from this study on promotional products.

- **84% of people remember the advertised business on the promotional item they receive.**
- 42% have a more favorable impression of a business after receiving a promotional item from them.
- *24% state that they are more likely to do business with an advertiser from the items they receive.*
- **62% have done business with the company or person they received a promotional item from.**
- Writing instruments are the most commonly-owned promotional items.
- **81% of promotional products are kept because they are considered useful.**
- More than three-quarters of respondents have had their items for about ten months and use them everyday.
- Bags were reported to be used most frequently, with respondents indicating that they use their bags on average nine times per month.
- **The average cost-per-impression of an advertising specialty item is $0.004, making it less expensive per impression than nearly any other media.** (According to Nielsen Media data, the CPI for a national magazine ad is $0.033; a newspaper ad is $0.0129; a prime time TV ad is $0.019; a cable TV ad is $0.007; a syndicated TV ad is $0.006; and a spot radio ad is $0.005)

Outrageous Promotions That Are Outrageously Effective

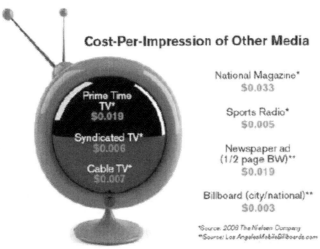

Chapter Four

All media is not created equal

In this chapter, we're going to compare the pros and cons of other media vs. promotional products in order to help you figure out the most cost effective media for your next marketing and advertising campaign.

Now if you're spending most of your marketing and advertising budget on Television, Radio, Newspaper and other print media now might be the time to reconsider your marketing mix and invest more in promotional products. It's a sure way to get a higher cost per impression and a bigger return on investment.

According to the study from ASI, promotional products perform better than all other types of marketing and advertising media including TV, print and radio when it comes to Cost Per Impression.

The ASI Study which includes interviews with more than 600 business people who had received promotional products shows that an astronomical 84% of the people that receive a promotional product can remember the advertisers on the branded promotional product they received up to one year ago.

Because the items are useful, they're kept and used frequently therefore repeating the marketing message many times over without any additional cost to the advertiser.

Try doing that with other media.

So let's take a few minutes to see why not all media is created equally.

Newspaper: A newspaper ad can get your message out to hundreds of thousands of readers but only a small percentage of those readers are your prospects and/or clients. These high priced ads are only good for one day: today's newspaper will end up in the recycling bin before the day is over. And let's not forget that your ad is competing with hundreds of other ads for the readers' attention.

Magazine/Trade Journals: These ads can be more targeted than other types of print media. However, readers buy magazines to gain information on a subject they are interested in or purely for entertainment. Magazine readers tend to quickly flip thru the ads in search of the next article. Most likely, your ad will be thorn out way before the next issue arrives.

Radio: Statistics show you need to run 8-10 spots a day for several days or weeks to create a successful radio campaign. Radio works best for consumer goods. But for business to business, the odds of your prospect needing your product when they hear your ad are minimal at best.

Television: The main problem with TV, other than the high cost, is the remote control. As soon as your commercial comes on the TV the channel surfing begins. TV can work great if you've got millions too spend of image advertising or brand building.

Billboards: Your message must be very brief so that it can be read at 65 MPH. The chances that you get your prospects attention and they pull out a pen to write your phone number down while driving are pretty much slim to none.

Pay Per Click/Search Engines: Your competitor's ad is right there next to yours. It's important to have a unique selling proposition

(USP) so that you can stand out from your competition. You're going to pay every time someone clicks on your ad so you had better make sure you have a dam good offer.

Direct Mail: Works GREAT if you target the right prospects. However even if you have the right mailing list you still have to get them to open it, read it and act on it. If you get creative with your direct mail efforts you can achieve a very high response rate and generate an outrageously high ROI.

As you can see from the above comparison, promotional products perform better than all other types of marketing and advertising media when it comes to Cost Per Impression (CPI).

Chapter Five:

The Impact, Exposure and Influence

When you want to make an impact and get your targets attention, nothing works better than promotional products because they are the only media that engages all five senses.

When you use promotional products, your customers and prospects can see, hear, touch, taste and even smell your message.

Once you start using promotional products as part of your marketing mix, you'll watch clients and prospects grab onto your message…and not let go.

And the reason they won't let go is because when properly selected promotional products serve a useful purpose to the target recipient.

Let's take a look at why they'll keep the promotional product in the first place.

LJ Market research and Glen Rich Business Studies conducted a study at Dallas Fort Worth Airport. The purpose of the study was to gain added knowledge about what "most" people do with promotional products and how they respond to the company they received them from.

So they went around the airport asking people… *"In the past 12 months have you received a promotional product?"*

- 71% of the 805 travelers interviewed actually owned at least one promotional product that they received in the past 12 months.

- 33% of this group had the item on their person... an extremely valuable location for your advertising.

When they asked..."*Can you name the company that gave you the promotional product?*"

- 76.1% could recall the name on the promotional product they had received as far back as 12 months ago.

- In comparison Airport subjects were asked if they had read a print publication in the previous week, 83% answered yes many of them on the flight yet only 53% could recall just one advertiser that appeared in the publication.

The percentage that could recall the advertiser on a promotional product they received in the last 12 months is 23% higher than the ability to recall an advertiser from a publication they read just in the previous week.

This clearly demonstrates the memory hook and long lasting impression created by the power of promotional products vs. print advertising.

- Of those that had received a promotional product, incredibly 100% could recall at least one item they had received.

- As many as 59% could recall at least two items and 30% could recall at least three items and 16% of them could recall up to four items.

- Wearables, writing instruments and desk/office accessories were the most frequently mentioned products; this finding is in line with the industry's top 3 product categories that we discussed earlier.

- The home followed by the office is the most popular location cited by the respondents.

I mention this and the top 3 products because when you select an item for your next promotion you want to keep these last two bullet points in mind.

The study was also designed to find out how long a person keeps a promotional product.

And what they found is **impossible** to achieve with any other media.

The study found that more than half 54% kept the item for more than a year. 31% kept the item for 6 months to a year.

When was the last time someone keep your print ad for more than a year…nothing personal but I'd have to say chance are as slim no fat milk.

The number one reason mentioned for keeping the item was the items usefulness. Followed by uniqueness and style. This is also one of those things to keep in mind when selecting an item for your next promotion.

Because the more useful the item is or the higher the perceived value of the item means they'll tend to be kept longer and used more frequently.

Outrageous Promotions That Are Outrageously Effective

Which increases your brand exposure and lowers your cost per impression.

Speaking of using frequently the study also found that as high as 45% used the promotional item on a daily basis. In addition, an astronomical 73% reported using the item at least once per week.

Case Study #1

> **These Products Really Help**
>
> Advertisers are the lifeblood of any magazine. However, in order to have advertisers they need to have consistent readers and loyal subscribers year after year. However when it comes to subscriptions literary magazines fall short because they cater to a specialized niche in the magazine market.
>
> The Missouri Review knew this when they wanted to increase its subscribers. "The promotion was to increase our web subscription sales for a three year subscription, because three year deals are always better for a magazine than a single year subscription," says Kris Somerville, Missouri Review marketing director. "Then we don't have to sign everyone back up every single year."
>
> The Missouri Review understands the power of promotional products. For several years, usually four or five times a year, they've been using promotional products to increase response rates to subscription promotions.
>
> "We believe if you give out a good product that seems too good to be true, people tend to subscribe," adds Somerville. "This audience doesn't like cheap trinkets. What they want is quality and functionality."
>
> This year the Missouri Review selected several products, which they offered depending on the subscription package. The products included a T-shirt, tote bag and coffee mug all branded with the magazine logo.

Outrageous Promotions That Are Outrageously Effective

> "It's been a success we've just been re-ordering the same products every three months and we're getting an average of one Web subscriber a day. We currently have a circulation of 5,000. For a literary magazine, that's a high number. These products really help with that."

This high frequency of use increases brand recall and is probably the number one reason 76% of the people can recall the advertisers name on the promotional product.

Unlike say Super Bowl ads that get the viewers raving about the ad but then when asked less than a week later they can't remember the advertiser's name.

I think this study proves a good point here because people do not remember most television, radio or print advertising and they sure don't keep and use other media the way they use promotional products.

As you get more into this book, you will learn how to select promotional products that not only will be kept and used but that the recipient will connect with and become attached to such as a stylish coffee mug that becomes "their mug". And let's not forget that a coffee mug can be seen at least 25 times a day.

Another great way to connect with your customers and/or prospects is with health or safety products because when the time comes that they need to use that first aid kit you gave them they'll be reminded of just how much you care about them.

We'll get more into that later in this book so before I go off on another tangent let me get back to what I was talking about.

So you know that when you give out the right promotional products your prospects and customers will keep, use and recall your company and your message.

But at the end of the day, what really matters is will people have a more favorable impression of your company and increase the likelihood doing business with you.

The survey showed that more than half (52%) of the people responded that they did business with the company after receiving the promotional product.

And as far as having a more favorable impression of the business, more than half said they have a more favorable opinion of the advertiser after receiving the promotional product.

They also said they were more likely to do business after receiving the promotional product.

This study proves the advantages promotional products offer that are not available with any other media:

- Highest recall rate over any other form of advertising
- Repeat exposure to the message
- Creates a favorable impression of the advertiser
- Engages the target audience while other media interrupts which increases the effectiveness of your advertising message.

I think you're starting to see the power of promotional products marketing but other than message recall let's take a look at the impact the power of promotional products has on brand awareness and brand image.

Because when it comes to increasing brand awareness, nothing does a better job than promotional products.

Chapter Six:

Brand Building and Company Image

In this chapter, we'll discuss several studies that can better show the impact promotional products have on a prospects and/or clients image of a company.

A study conducted by Baylor University shows how promotional products can create goodwill and positive feeling towards a business.

For the study, they used a textbook publisher to send out to 4,000 educators

1) A letter with a pocket calculator
2) A letter with a lower priced product; a highlighter
3) A letter alone

So what did the findings reveal and what can we learn from it?

The findings revealed that the ones that received the letter with a promotional product expressed more good will toward the company and its salespeople than those that didn't receive a promo product with the letter.

In chapter 10, I'm going to show you how you should be using the *Promotional Products That Works* concept to increase the effectiveness of your direct mail campaigns.

Something else to consider when selecting promotional product is that the attitudes of those who received the calculator, which has a higher perceived value, were consistently more positive than those who received the less expensive highlighter.

And as high as 54% more positive than the ones that got the letter only.

If you're reading this book, you're probably looking for smart ways to enhance and increase your brand awareness.

However, after reading this chapter you should also be looking for ways to use promotional products to create goodwill and positive feeling towards your company.

Okay but I know what you're really thinking. You're thinking that's wonderful but how does all this goodwill and all these positive feelings benefit your business?

Good question!

So let me tell you about the amazing result discovered by Dr. Kathleen Gruben. She put participants in an experimental group that received a promotional product with the logo of a local restaurant. The control group received nothing.

30 days later, she asked questions to determine the differences between the two group's images of the restaurant.

The group that received a promotional product had a significantly more positive overall image of the café than the control group.

What she found was truly amazing…99.2% of the group that received the promotional product was more likely to talk about and make positive comments about the restaurant even though most had never been to the restaurant.

They were also significantly more likely to recommend the restaurant than the group that received nothing.

Again, remember they are recommending a restaurant they've never been to based solely on the perception created by the power of promotional products!

That's a powerful way to make a first impression.

I think it's safe to say that the power of promotional products will create a positive impact on your brand image.

The research clearly shows that people who receive a promotional product have a significantly more positive opinion about a business as well as…

- A more positive overall image
- A more positive perception of the business
- A higher likelihood of recommending the business
- A higher likelihood of patronizing the business

Especially when comparing people who receive a promotional product from a company with others who do not.

The restaurant in this study experienced a positive impact on its brand that has lead to an increase in new customers and an increase of 15 – 20% in sales to the point that they opened a second restaurant a few months after the study.

And yes they continue to use promotional products as part of their marketing.

Outrageous Promotions That Are Outrageously Effective

So, how's that for a quantifiable way to prove the powerful impact that promotional products can have on your business.

It's truly amazing the results that can be achieved using the power of promotional products marketing.

CASE STUDY #2

> This past winter the Newton Athletic Club was looking for a practical but unique thank you gift to give its members. The Newton Athletic Club offers wellness programs for adults and kids as well as an onsite spa, salon and daycare.
>
> Between the daycare center and the kids' wellness programs, the club has hundreds of kids. During the winter months that adds up to a whole lot of runny noses. The tissue cup dispenser was the perfect promotional product for the gym to give its members during the winter months. In addition, the tissue cup design, which is meant to fit in cars cup holder, made it a practical and unique gift.
>
> The tissue cup showed members that they gym cared about them because they understood that during Flu season people were always reaching for a tissue whether in the gym or in the car. It's a sign that they went the extra mile to help their members. They gave out 1,000 branded tissue cups to members as they checked in. The objective of the promotion was to create goodwill and loyalty among the members of the club during flu season…Mission Accomplished!

I hope that by now you are starting to see how all those positive feelings might have a positive and profitable impact on your company image.

Plus using promotional products also offers you a terrific advantage in terms of brand awareness. While the big guys have the money to spend on endless TV spots and full page print ads for brand awareness you can utilize promotional products to create brand awareness at a fraction of the cost.

See every time you use a promotional product imprinted with your company logo you are building brand awareness. This is what I call the "Side Effect" of promotional products marketing.

The "Side Effects" of using promotional products as a part of your marketing is that it lets builds and reinforces your brand. Brand building alone is extremely expensive but with promo products, it's a free side effect.

This happens because once they accept the promotional product…they start a relationship with the brand. That relationship will continue throughout the useful life of the product. Your brand is reinforced several times a day in that persons mind as they use your promotional product.

Keep in mind how powerful promotional products marketing really is. With other media your brand exposure ends the minute your TV or radio ad ends.

With print media the brand exposure begins when they see it and ends the second they flip the page or look away.

But if you select the right promotional product your brand exposure continues to build for months and even years.

Promotional products have the unique advantage to engage your target audience. Unlike traditional media that interrupts, promotional products engage the recipients.

Since I've gone off on a tangent about brand building, I want to point out to you just like I do to all of my clients that promo products levels the playing field between you and the big fortune 500.

Because when it comes to brand building any size business big or small can afford to use the same promotional products.

So you can in essence give the impression that you're a much larger company. I believe this has a lot to do with why the studies show that people have a much more favorable impression of a business that uses promotional products.

Keep this in mind as you start thinking about creating a *Promotional Products That Work* marketing campaign.

When you select a promotional product for your campaign always think how will this product represents my brand.

Since you can afford to imprint your brand on any promotional product that the bigger companies use then think to yourself would they use this item?

There are many other ways to put the power of promotional products to work such as generating referrals, increasing traffic to a tradeshow booth or increasing response rates to direct mail and other forms of advertising.

But for now lets talk about how you can use the power of promotional products to increase referrals, which will create more business.

Chapter Seven:

Increase referrals

We've all heard the old adage that it cost something like 9-12 times more to sell to a new customer than to existing customers.

I'm sure you've also heard that there is a higher closing ratio with leads that are referrals then with cold leads.

There is no better place to get referrals than from existing customer.

You should look at them as a referral gold mine.

Therefore, you need to keep them motivated to give referrals.

Using the power of promotional products as an incentive you can leverage customer satisfaction and secure more valuable referrals.

Promotional products will help motivate your customers to provide you with the names of friends and associates that you could do business with.

A study done by Baylor University reveals that customers who received promotional products are more willing to provide referrals vs. customers who don't receive promotional products.

They gave promo products to one group of customers along with a request for referrals and the other group just received a request for referrals with no promotional product.

The study found that the customers who received a promotional product gave 22% more referral leads than those who received nothing.

Think about what 22% more referrals would mean for your business.

Providing promotional gifts to customers will increase the likelihood of them providing your sales people with business referrals, which will increase the number of leads generated.

Using the power of promotional products to create a referral promotion to expand your customer base will insure the continuous growth of your business; promotional products are the most effective tool available for growing your referral leads.

Case Study #3

> **Each Quarter They Receive Dozens of Referrals As A Result Of The Promotion**
>
> When Exclusively Yours, a consulting firm wanted to increase referrals they turned to the power of promotional products. They created a referral program around the personalized business approach they practice. They selected items that were soft and would create a sense of comfort and warmth.
>
> They launched their referral promotion in early spring when nights are still a bit nippy so they chose a fleece blanket that rolled up with a Velcro strap and handle. The blanket was beautifully embroidered with the company logo. The blankets were sent out whenever they received a referral accompanied with a note that read, "Your referral gives us a warm fuzzy feeling."
>
> The referral promotion was so successful they created another theme for the summer. They chose plush bears with the message "Thank you beary much for your referral." And for the winter flu season they

> created a gift basket with soup packets, imprinted mugs, antibacterial tissues and hand sanitizer gel.
>
> Each quarter they received dozens of referrals because of the referral promotion. One client has been giving them one new referral every week. They estimate $1,000 to $5,000 worth of business from each referral that becomes a new client.

And as I mentioned earlier we all know that it's more profitable to sell to an existing customer than a new customer. And that's why the business world relies heavily on building and maintaining current relationships as well as fostering new ones.

One of the best ways to keep customers loyal to your business is to thank them for their business and keep in touch with them on a consistent basis.

To do this you can create a multi-sequence "Touch" campaign.

Let me tell you about a commercial lender that does a truly remarkable job of keeping customers loyal and separates themselves from other lenders in their market.

Plus generates an endless flow of referrals!

They have created a 7-step touch system. Included in their system is the use of promotional products as gifts that are mailed out periodically.

The promotional products are intended to not only reward but also to create brand loyalty by selecting gifts that the client will personally use and keep in their home or office.

Step 1 is the "flashlight letter." Once a client has committed to working with them, they congratulate them for making that choice.

Outrageous Promotions That Are Outrageously Effective

Within a day or two new clients, receive via priority mail a Mag-Lite flashlight branded with the company logo and their 800 number.

They include a letter with the headline "Congratulations….You've seen the light!" The letter goes on to congratulate them for their enlightened decision.

<u>Step 2</u> is the "clock letter." This is also sent via priority mail and it includes an analog desk clock with their company name and phone number on the base of the clock. The clock along with the letter acknowledges the importance of time during the transaction.

<u>Step 3</u> The stress check ruler letter. The next step in the loan process is getting the file to the underwriting department. The day the file goes to underwriting they send out a letter letting the client know that the file has been sent to underwriting.

The headline reads…"Stress Reliever Enclosed….Warning—Waiting for formal loan approval may be stressful" They include a white plastic ruler with a fun to use stress sensor on the front. The stress sensor measures the heat and moisture from a person's finger and then changes to a color equal to their stress level.

<u>Step 4</u> The portfolio pouch letter. Notifying the client that the loan has been approved is perhaps the most important and most enjoyable part of the loan process.

Upon loan approval, they send out a leather portfolio pouch with the company logo along with a letter encouraging the client to store all legal documents in the portfolio.

<u>Step 5</u> The personalized thank you card. A day after the loan closes they send out a very unique thank you card. The card has a very

personalized message on the inside and goes on to inform the client that they'll be receiving another gift in the mail shortly.

Step 6 The gift basket. With in a week of closing the loan the client receives a very nice gift basket of fruits, chesses and wines. The basket comes with a small thank you card tied with a ribbon printed with the company logo.

Step 7 The referral and testimonial request. Two to three days after receiving the gift basket they send out a laser engraved pen along with a letter requesting referrals and a testimonial form the client.

The timing is perfect because the client has had a unique experience as well as feels obligated because of all the gifts they have received.

Their response rate is well over 50%, which provides them with a steady stream of new potential clients and an arsenal of testimonial to use in their marketing.

Amazing!

So you may be thinking how can they afford to do this or even trying to figure out if you can afford to do something like this for your clients.

If you add up the cost of all the gifts, including postage, and printing of the letters, they're spending about $125 per client.

Their average collected fee on a loan is $7,000 -$9,000 so you be the judge as to whether they can afford to use this system.

Also, consider the lifetime value of each satisfied and loyal client. And don't forget to consider the $7,000 - $9,000 value of all the referrals they generate using this system.

Using the power of promotional product as business gifts is a great way to show your clients how much you value their business and it will create brand loyalty that can last a lifetime.

There you have it...without a doubt the power of *Promotional Products That Work* will motivate your customers to provide you with the names of friends and associates that you could do business with.

Cool stuff...this chapter alone can change your business!

Chapter Eight:

MORE SALES = MORE REVENUE!

Customers who receive promotional products on average return sooner and more frequently and spend more money than customers who receive just coupons and discounts.

In two separate studies performed by Southern Methodist University, researchers show that promotional products outperform coupons in the area of repeat business and sales.

Study One: New Customers
- Over an eight-month period, new customers that received promotional products spent 139% more than those who received only a welcome letter did and 27% more than those who received just coupons.
- They were also 75% more likely than letter only recipients to patronize the business and 49% more likely than coupon recipients were.

Study Two: Existing Customers
- Customers who received promotional products reordered up to 18% sooner than those who received coupons.
- Customers who received promotional products also averaged up to 18% more orders than those receiving coupons.

Both studies show that customers who received promotional products reordered more quickly and more often than those receiving no promotional products did.

Both studies can't be wrong.

Plain and simple using promotional products means more sales and more revenue.

Dr. Richard Beltramini of Wayne State University demonstrated that using promotional products as "Thank You" gifts significantly improved both sales and customer loyalty.

Beltramini accomplished this by comparing results across three groups:

1) The letter group received only a letter of thanks
2) The "Silver Group" received the letter plus a sliver desk set ($20 retail value)
3) The "Gold Group" received the letter plus a gold desk set ($40 retail value)

- Those who received the gold & silver 'thank you" gifts were 43% and 23% more satisfied with the company than those who received only a thank you letter.

- Silver and gold gift recipients "intent to buy" ratings were higher than the letter only recipients.

- Even six months after the "thank you" gifts were distributed, sales for the silver and gold groups were 400% higher than sales for the letter only group.

- While both the silver and gold "thank you" gifts had a significant impact on both positive attitude and buying behavior, the gold group because of the higher perceived value of the gift did have a much greater impact than the silver group.

Case Study #4

> As the holiday season was approaching, a Houston, Texas distributor was looking for a gift to give clients that would also help them increase future business. They selected an assortment of gifts that included a classic coaster set, a stainless steel candle set, a shoeshine kit, the Icon action dice set and the Zagat gourmet gift set.
>
> The result was incredible and more than they hoped for. They generated an enormous amount of goodwill and a big increase in business. In the first quarter of the New Year, they generated an additional $100,000 in sales from their top customers. When properly planned and thought out the power of promotional products can produce outrageous result even for a small business.

In summary customers that receive "thank you" gifts will have a more positive attitude towards a business and will buy more often.

And when determining your budget for thank you gifts remember that the higher the perceived value of the gift the greater the impact will be on your sales.

Chapter Nine: Trade Shows

MORE TRAFFIC = MORE LEADS

Tradeshows are one of the most important components of the overall marketing mix for many companies. Tradeshows are one of the best ways to connect buyers and sellers because of the face-to-face interaction.

Exhibiting at tradeshows can be expensive but promotional products can play a key role in making sure you get the highest ROI.

One of the best ways to increase your ROI is to increase the traffic to your tradeshow booth. Tradeshow professionals all agree that promotional products are extremely effective traffic drivers.

The greater the traffic, the greater the number of sales leads generated.

Having giveaway items at the tradeshow is very important. Nowadays you can't attend a tradeshow and not walk out with bags full of promotional giveaways.

While this is a smart thing for exhibitors to do most tend to overlook the most vital part of tradeshow marketing and that is the pre-show marketing.

Therefore, the first thing we need to talk about is pre-show marketing.

Using the power of promotional products in conjunction with pre-show marketing makes an effective tool to inform, remind and persuade attendees to visit your booth

A study conducted by Georgia Southern University proved that including a pre-show mailing with a promo product or an offer of a promotional product will increase the number of attendees stopping by your tradeshow booth.

In fact, a pre-show gift can produce three times more traffic to a booth than an invitation alone.

A sampling of pre-registered attendees was drawn from a total list of over 2,000. They were divided into 3 groups.

Group A: received an invitation postcard inviting the recipient to stop by the exhibitors booth.

Group B: received an invitation postcard along with an inexpensive promotional magnet custom printed with the exhibitors logo and booth number.

Group C: received an invitation postcard and an offer for a free T-shirt for visiting the exhibitors booth.

At this point in the book, I hope you can guess the outcome of this study.

Yes, the postcard invitation with the offer for a free T-shirt out pulled all the others.

The study results showed a very impressive 78% more people responded with the free t-shirt offer than the postcard alone.

And 56% more people responded to the postcard and magnet than the postcard alone.

So including a promotional product with your pre-show mailing will significantly increase the response rate to your invitation to visit your booth.

What would it mean for your company if you could increase traffic to your tradeshow booth by 78%?

Case Study #5

> Citect knows you've got to play the marketing game but the amount they had to play with was limited. They used their limited budget wisely and planned a hotel room drop promotion for a trade show in Vegas. They intended to drive traffic to their both by holding a drawing for a poker set.
> Because the budget was limited, they used stock poker-chip printed chocolates to place on pillows in the hotel rooms of attendees. They presented the chocolates with a deck of cards. They packaged the card decks along with marketing collateral about Citect inside a velour bag that would keep everything neatly inside and make the gifts easy to distribute.
> As attendees arrived at their hotel rooms, they found the bag with a shinny reflex blue foil printed with the tag line "Beat The Odds with Citect" this further supported the theme and reinforced the brands awareness.
> Inside they received the branded card decks, the chocolate poker chips and a card that needed to be filled out and dropped off at the Citect booth for a chance to win the poker set.
> The promotion was a true winner. Many people stopped by the booth to drop off their cards and thank them for the gift bag. Citect

> feels they made a lasting impression and the packaging enhanced the perceived value of the brand.

One of the best ways to increase traffic to your booth is to use a two-part promotion.

A simple example of what I mean is that you can mail out your invitation along with a set of headphones and ask them to come by your booth to receive an MP3 Player. You can send out one part of a pen and pencil set or a coaster with an offer for a mug. You get the point.

The goal is to get the recipients to come by your booth to claim the second part of their gift. By the way a two-part promotion isn't just for tradeshows it's also a great way to set-up appointments.

Once they show up at your booth, you should have promotional products to give them. But I encourage my clients to find a better way of handing out promotional products.

First, I always encourage my clients to define the demographics of their target market. By going thru the demographics of your target audience, you can narrow down the specific products that appeal to your target market and fit your budget.

As a rule of thumb the greater the perceived value of the promotional products the greater the number of sales leads it will generate. Notice that I said the perceived value not the actual value.

What I suggest my clients do to help stay within budget and appeal to their target market is to have three different levels of promotional products to give out at their booth.

So instead of spending your entire budget on one item you should divide up your budget among three price points. Let me give you an example of a tiered trade show budget. Of course these number will vary depending on your budget and your market.

Level 1 The Masses: One low priced item for the masses AKA the freebie seekers. An item between $0.50- $2.00 and depending on the size of the show 500 to 1,000 pieces is good.

Level 2 The Decision Influencers: A mid-priced promotional gift in the $2.50 - $ $5.00 range in the quantity of 250 – 500

Level 3 The Decision Makers: An item with a high perceived value in the range of $5.00 - $10.00 in the quantity of 100 – 250.

So let's say you have a $1,500 budget. Instead of getting 1500 pieces of a $1.00, item what I recommend as the smart thing to do is break down your budget into the three levels.

Level 1 gets 500 items at $0.50 each for a total of $250.00
Level 2 gets 250 items at $2.50 each for a total of $625.00
Level 3 gets 100 items at $5.00 each for a total of $500.00

Your total comes to $1,375, which leaves $125 for set-up fees and shipping charges. When figuring out your budget, don't forget to leave some room for set-up charges and shipping cost.

Understanding your target markets demographic will help you select an item that will appeal to your target market. And using the three level price points will help you get a bigger bang for your tradeshow buck.

So you might be thinking just how effective are promotional products as giveaways at tradeshows?

Georgia Southern University examined how promotional products impact a recipient's perception of a company and their products and/or service.

The study was performed at four tradeshows. What they did was collect data through exit surveys designed to determine what attendees remembered about the promotional products they received at the trade show and their impression of the company giving them out.

What they found is that 71% of attendees who received a promotional product remembered the name of the company that gave them the product.

And 76% of the attendees left the tradeshow with a favorable attitude toward the company that gave them the product.

Providing promotional products to attendees at tradeshows significantly increases the likelihood of them remembering your company and creates a much more favorable image of your company in their minds.

As you can see promotional products are a very important component to help you make your tradeshow marketing more effective and to help increase your ROI.

So apply what you've learned in this chapter and incorporate promotional products at your next tradeshow by creating a special promotion designed to increase traffic to your booth and create a positive image of your company.

And don't forget about your pre-show marketing. By simply mailing a relevant promotional product to your target market before the show, you can create a consistent flow of visitors to your booth without breaking the bank.

With a well-planned tradeshow promotion, a company can easily generate hundreds of leads. However, all that effort is wasted if there isn't a post show follow up marketing plan.

What I strongly suggest to my clients is that they follow up with all the leads they generate at the tradeshow. But the thing to do is to identify your top 50 to 100 prospects.

Once you know who your top prospects are then send them a personalized mailing. You can use a portfolio personalized with their name and enclose your company brochure, sales letter, offer, etc in one pocket along with a hand written "Nice meeting you" note.

The best way to follow up with all the other leads is to create a multi step direct mail follow up campaign.

In the next chapter, we're going to discuss how to use promotional products to make your mailings much more effective. But first let me give you an example of a very effective multi step direct mail campaign.

Case Study #6

> Promotion Creates More New Business
> Than Sales Consultant Can Handle!
> How does the New York Times bestselling author of the book *The Ultimate Sales Machine* get new sales? I'm talking about the incredibly successful sales trainer and consultant Chet Holmes and he uses the power of promotional products!
> Holmes says, "Basically what we do is pick out our dream clients. The ones that we'd love to work with and we send them one of these

little promotional gifts every week for six weeks straight. The when you call them, they get right on the phone."

Holmes dream list consist of names from the fastest growing INC 500, the entire fortune 1,000, close to 200 industry associations and some hand picked smaller businesses. In order to promote his latest book he sent the dream list a multi-part mailing. First, he sent out an orange calculator (keeping with the color of the book) with a sales letter that read, "You're going to need an extra calculator to calculate your sales increase, once you apply the concepts in the new book, *The Ultimate Sales Machine.*"

The mailing was followed with a high-liter, a shoe polish kit, a magnifying glass, etc all with a corresponding tag line that referred to his book. Holmes said he received numerous calls not only to buy the book but also to schedule consultations. "I'm expecting to get more new business than we can handle. You know in all honesty my time will probably be sold out and I'll just have to keep raising my prices." If you would like a free preview of chapter four of *The Ultimate Sales Machine* simply visit chetholmes.com/book.

Chapter Ten:

Direct Mail

In this chapter, I'm going to show you how to not only dramatically increase the number of direct mail pieces that get opened but you'll also see your response rates go through the roof as a result.

This is done using the power of *Promotional Products That Work* to create what I call "Gotta Know Mail". Others refer to it as lumpy mail or 3-d mail because including a promotional product makes the mail piece lumpy.

But the real magic isn't in the lump it's in the curiosity that it creates. The recipient is "Gotta Know" what's in there.

"Gotta Know" mail works great because their curiosity gets the best of them and before they know it, they are opening your envelope before all the others.

The best sales letter or direct mail packages in the world will not do you any good if you can't get them to open the envelope.

Over the years, the direct mail industry along with the postal service has conducted studies to figure out how people open their mail. The studies show that people first open what looks like personal mail, then bills, and then finally they look at advertising mail and generally, whatever looks like out right junk mail goes right into the trashcan.

"Gotta Know" mail doesn't fit into any of the preconceived categories that the brain has created to sort mail so it ends up grabbing the attention of your prospect and being opened first.

This is also called the Cracker Jack effect referring to the Cracker Jacks snack box with the toy gift inside.

Another psychological effect of including a promotional product with your mailing is reciprocity. This is a very powerful psychological trigger because of the process that takes place in a persons mind after receiving something for free.

They immediately feel obligated to return the favor. This is the reason why as we saw in previous chapters giving promotional products as business gifts and thank you gifts is so powerful.

It's also the reason promotional products are so effective in the tradeshow setting.

As the saying goes, it is better to give than to receive.

The psychology of reciprocity makes your prospects more open to actually paying attention to your message and doing whatever you've directed them to in your call to action.

This means you will see an increase in response rates which will mean more appointments set, more return phone calls and of course more sales and more profits. You can learn more about this from Dr. Cialdinis book The Power of Influence.

I truly love to use the direct response strategies that I've learned from mentors like Dan Kennedy and Bill Glazer to find ways for my clients to combine the power of promotional products with their direct mail campaigns to increase their open rates, response rates and ROI.

I'm going to tell you about a study conducted by Baylor University to help you more vividly see the power of promotional products when combined with direct mail.

In this study, one group received sales literature alone. A second group received sales literature along with a hi-liter. And a third group received the same sales literature with a hi-liter along with an offer of a more expensive gift (a desktop calculator) for responding.

I'm sure that by now you can probably figure out the results of this study.

Correct…Those who received the Hi-Liter responded at a rate that was 57% higher than those who received just the sales letter.

Response rate for the incentive of a free gift offer, which was the higher perceived value desktop calculator, was 75% higher than the group who received only the sales literature.

Because of the higher response rate, the cost per response was lowered by 66%.

I know from my years in this industry that quite a few people reading this might be thinking that it cost more to include a promotional product with their direct mail.

So I'm going to take a few minutes to go over how the additional cost is absorbed by the increased response rate.

Let's assume for a minute that your product or service sells for $299.00.

Now let's say that you're mailing out 1,000 sales letters and the cost of doing that is $590 and that includes the letter, the envelope and the postage.

If you're getting the standard 1% response rate, which equals 10 buyers at $299 you're bringing in $2,999.00 for every 1,000 pieces you, mail out which equals a $2,409.00 return on investment.

Now let's add a promotional product that cost $1.00. The cost of your mailing is now $1,590.00 that includes the letter, the envelope, the postage and the promotional product.

If you increase your response rate by just 1% for a response rate of 2% which equals 20 sales at $299 that means you bring in $5,980.00 for every 1,000 piece you mail out which equals a $4,390.00 return on investment for the same 1,000 letters.

So while your cost went up by $1 your return on investment almost doubled and you also doubled the number of prospects turned into buying customers.

When you factor in the lifetime value of the 20 new customers your return on investment skyrockets.

If your average customer buys from you once a year for an average of three years the lifetime value (LTV) of each new customer is $897 ($299 x 3 years = $897.00)

So let me ask you this question... would you rather gain 10 new customer per thousand piece mailed for a LTV of $8,970.00 (10 x $897.00 = $8,970.00) or would you rather get 20 new customers for every 1,000 pieces mailed out for a LTV of $17,940.00 (20 x $897.00 = $17,940.00)

Outrageous Promotions That Are Outrageously Effective

I have yet to come across one single business that would not want to double their response rate, double their return on investment and double their LTV because they had to invest an extra $1 in their direct mail campaign.

Case Study #7

> ### Custom Promotion Yields 33% Response Rate
>
> Detweiler, Hershey & Associated is not your typical accounting firm. When the time came for the firm to introduce new wealth management services to its client base they wanted to do it with a promotional campaign that would stand out from the usual promotional products that financial services firms tend to give out. They arrived at this decision because the more typical mailings they had done in the past did not yield the results they hoped for. The firm in the last few years had been offering clients seminars with little to no response. They would spend hundreds of dollars to send out traditional invitations and produce a very small or no return on investment.
>
> This time around, the firm went with a much more dramatic approach. They mailed out a decorative box with full color printed flyers to its 99 largest clients. The marketing literature gave them the details about a free seminar including the benefits of attending and how to register for the seminar. To pique interest a teaser tag line read, "Stressed over your finances? Help is just a phone call away." To further drive the theme and provide recipients with a tangible reminder they included a stress reliever shaped as a cell phone printed with the firm logo. The firm says the promotion was astounding. A third of the recipients responded to the invitation to attend the seminar, four scheduled appointments and three signed up for the new wealth management service before even attending the seminar. The campaign, which cost about $1,800 including shipping and handling, more than paid for itself. The firm was so impressed with

> the result they did a second campaign using the same format to other clients. This time they placed a branded coaster with the message "We can handle your liquid assets." The firm believes that using the power of promotional products is a solid investment.

When you offer a free gift as an incentive to respond you can use the free gift to track your response rate. I don't recommend ordering the free promotional gift until the responses start coming in.

Once you know how many responses you have then order only what you need to fulfill the free gift offer. Using this method is one of the best ways of tracking your response rate because you know exactly how many people responded to your offer by how many items you need to order. This also prevents any waste in over ordering.

In a nutshell promotional products can be used to create "gotta know" or lumpy mail which significantly increases your open rates.

The promotional product is also used to motivate a call to action from the prospect as an easy way to track and measure the results of the mailing.

Chapter Eleven:

Does your marketing interrupt or engage?

In this chapter, we're going to talk about how you can also use promotional products as a way to measure the results of other advertising mediums like TV, radio, newspaper and magazines or even online marketing efforts.

You can use the power of promotional products to test and measure the results of your TV, Radio and Print by simply tying in an offer of a promotional product as an incentive to respond.

And for the first time ever you'll have an effective way to measure the results of all your media. For example in TV, Radio or Print Ad you could offer a free sleeve of golf balls

"Stop by today and get a free sleeve of golf balls"

If enough people come in and ask for a free sleeve of golf balls, you can tell if the media is pulling, if no one responds test a different offer. If you still get a low response than you need to try a different media.

I always advise all my clients running TV, radio or any other media spots to test, test, test, and the easiest way to test is using promotional products as incentives to respond.

Lets also talk about the impact promotional products can have on other media. When you combine promotional products with other media it can increases brand interest by as much as 69%.

The University of Texas and Louisiana State University designed a study to measure:

- The effectiveness of promo products and compared them to two other media, TV and print.
- The synergistic effects of promo products when used along with these other media
- The consumers preferred medium for information about a product or brand.

The participants in the study were exposed to three forms of advertising…TV, Print, and promo products.

All in all the study revealed that all groups who were exposed to promotional products rated the advertising message more favorably than those groups who were not exposed to any promotional products.

The study proves that the addition of promotional products actually increases favorability ratings towards the ads.

In terms of positive attitude towards the ad, a promotional product to the media mix generates a favorable attitude towards the ad in all cases by 44%.

Respondents scored promotional products at 44% vs. TV ads, which they scored at only 18%.

In terms of message credibility, promotional products scored 54% vs. 33% for TV.

And for purchase intent, promotional products came in at 25% vs. 17% for TV.

Lastly, for referral value promotional products beat the TV ad with 26% vs. 16%.

In this study, the groups that were exposed to promotional products tended to overwhelmingly rate the message more positively than those groups not exposed to a promo product.

So now you know that adding the power of promotional product to the media mix will generate a favorable attitude towards the ad in all cases.

In some instances, the use of a promo product as the ad medium alone achieved the greatest impact with up to 69% in increasing brand interest and 84% in creating a good impression of the brand.

So not only should you be using the power promotional products to test and measure your TV and print ads but you should also be using it to generate a more favorable attitude towards your ads.

I always suggest testing because you might discover that promo products marketing alone can produce the same if not better results for your marketing dollars.

Let me share with you the story of a The Aspen Hills Tennis Club.

The tennis club was running television ads (at a cost of $5,000) as a way to recruit new members. When they ran the campaign they would generate about 100 responses. Of those 100 responses, they would secure two new members.

$5,000 divided by two new members = $2,500 to secure each new member.

The marketing director would justify this high acquisition cost because the annual membership fee was $3,000 and the average lifetime of a member was 6 years.

The average lifetime value (LTV) of each new member was $18,000 (6 years x $3,000 per year) when you add in the $500 net profit from the TV ads the campaign would create a potential $37,000 in lifetime revenue.

However, I know that using the power of promotional products the tennis club could get a significantly higher return on investment.

The first thing is to understand the demographics of the tennis clubs target market…35 to 55 year old males and females with a high median income that played tennis and lived within a 50 mile radius.

With the help of list broker, the Aspen Hills Tennis Club acquired a list 300 of qualified prospects.

They created a custom box for a direct marketing campaign.

The printing on the outside of the box read

"The Aspen Hill Tennis Club is serving up a great offer…"

Once the box was opened, the message continued,

"Now the balls in your court"

The inside of the box was die-cut. Inside they inserted a tennis ball along with a personalized free week membership card.

Additional copy printed inside the box described the clubs features.

The offer was an invitation to try the club for one week, a free "Test Drive" to play tennis, meet the members and experience the club first hand.

To their surprise, the marketing campaign generated an amazing 25% response rate.

75 people signed up for the free week. After the free week, 54 people signed up for memberships.

The marketing campaign used the same $5,000 budget that was used to run the TV spots but generated an astronomical increase in new memberships.

The ROI generated by this campaign in comparison to the TV ad was astronomical.

$5,000 divided by 300 = $16.66 per prospect

54 new members: $5,000 divided by 54 = $92.59 to secure each new member instead of $2,500

New member fee $3,000 X 54 = $162,000

$162,000 minus the $5,000 investment gives you a $157,000 net profit. That brings the ROI to just over 3,100%

That kind of return on investment puts a real serious whopping on the result generated by the TV spots.

But lets not forget that we still haven't added up the LTV of each new member = $18,000 (6 years X $3,000 per year)

LTV of 54 new members = $972,000

With a net profit of $157,000 and a LTV of $972,000 that brings the revenue created by this $5,000 dollar marketing campaign to $1,129,000 dollars.

That's an ROI of over 22,000%

I guarantee you this tennis club never again ran a TV campaign. I'll bet they stopped taking the sales reps calls.

While these results may sound unbelievable, I can assure you that the businesses that have discovered the power of *Promotional Products That Work* are generating these kinds of outrageous returns with each and every promotional products campaign they create.

I know most people can't even get their heads around these kinds of results.

They just don't believe this is possible or maybe they believe it isn't possible for them to achieve these kinds of results.

And that my friend is the reason why I wrote this book. I hope that by now we can say we're friends.

The results are so phenomenal that they may sound too good to be true. And that's why I've included the results of so many studies.

Believe me I wasn't trying to bore you to death with facts and studies.

But like I said in the beginning of this book no other marketing medium is victim to so much misunderstanding, mis-education and misuse as promotional products.

Therefore, I needed to give you the proof. And not only did I give you the proof but I also showed you first hand results from companies big and small that are putting the power of *Promotional Products That Work* creating outrageous promotions and marketing campaigns that are killing their competitors.

It's not my intention to brag about the kind of results that I've created for my clients.

What I hope is that reading these examples will give you some ideas to swipe and use for your business.

My goal is to give you the confidence to know that you to can use the power of *Promotional Products That Work* to transform your marketing and your business.

I promised that I would give you the knowledge and the tools. I think I've more than lived up to my end of the deal.

Now its time for you to use the knowledge and the tools to explode your profits.

After you've read the book and gone thru all the outrageous promotions swipe file in the next section, I would strongly recommend that you get our Outrageous Promotions Planning Guide. Available at www.outrageouspromotions.net or by giving us a quick call at 305-888-7301.

This is the best and easiest tool to help you create outrageous promotions and marketing campaigns that can achieve the same if not better results than the ones you've read about in this book.

So let's move on to the outrageous promotions swipe file. Read thru all of these real-life case studies with an open-mind.

Don't just read the ones you think only apply to your business because with an open-mind, the strategies that you've discovered in this book and a little creativity you to can create an outrageous promotions that outrageously effective!

Section Two:

Outrageous Promotions Swipe File

The CAMPAIGN Created A 100% RESPONSE RATE

Imagine finding a safe in your mailbox. That's exactly what happened all around the country as 170 executives of trucking companies got their mail. Inside the safe they could hear something rattling around. By reading the postcard included in the mailing the executives were instructed to visit a website to discover the combination to open the safe.

Once the safe was opened inside they found a silver dollar plus information about the company; Bergstrom Inc which manufactures a battery powered no-idle thermal environment product that could help them save thousands of dollars a year in fuel cost.

The goal was to drive home the issue of cost savings as trucking companies continue to get slammed with rising diesel fuel cost and pressured to stop long periods of engine idling as an environmental concern. The power of promotional products helped convey the cost savings message and makes it easier for companies to understand the benefit.

Using the power of promotional products the campaign created a 100% response rate. That's right all 170 recipients responded to the mailing. The campaigns success is due in large part to the curiosity factor created by the safe. Once opened the accompanying marketing collateral feed that curiosity. Creatively tying in the power of promo products not only got them 100% response rate but about 25% passed along the info to colleagues in the industry.

Within the first week; two of the companies that received the promotion purchased units. To date 100 units have been sold as direct result of the promotion. The promotion more than paid for itself. The Return on Investment (ROI) was measurable and in a time when marketing dollars are tight it's wonderful to generate such a big ROI.

12% Response Rate & Revenue EXCEEDING $108 MILLION

Playground Destinations understands that it's crucial to create interest in prospective buyers. So when it came time to start planning the sale of its latest property; Laua Resort Condominiums in Sandestin, Fl they knew they needed a great promotion in order to sell 223 units at an average price of $450,000.

Playground Destinations enlisted the power of promotional products to meet their objective of pre-selling the luxury condo units to interested prospects. They developed a direct mail campaign that incorporated beach  sand and seashells along with a "New Owner Appreciation Kit". The incentive gift generated an almost 12% response rate. On sales day all 223 units were sold creating revenue exceeding $108 Million in purchase agreements. To further reinforce the Laua Resort brand condo buyers were rewarded with The "New Owner Appreciation Kit".

The kit consisted of custom branded beach sandals, two beach towels and a beach bag packaged inside a rolling beach cooler. Using the power of promotional products was a nice touch to give new buyers a glimpse of their future life on the beach.

FINALLY They Returned My Call

The news, entertainment and advertising on more than 7,000 digital screens in elevators inside office buildings across the country are provided by The Captivate Network. The Captivate Network wanted to get their sales reps in front of Chief Marketing Officers, media planners and ad agency people. Their goal is to try to get Captivate as part of these peoples marketing mix.

The idea came about to use a deck of cards printed with tongue-in-cheek "Elevator Meditations". Too deliver the cards a special card stock packaging was created. The package was printed with a "elevator meditation guru" on the front cover. When the package flips open inside you find elevator doors and a pull tab. When you pull the tab, the elevator doors open and inside you find the deck of cards.

The over 4% response was phenomenal considering there was no real call to action. The promotion sent recipients to a special website www.elevatormeditations.com. Levy a sales rep for Captivate says "We've gotten amazing calls and emails- from people that I've been trying to met forever. Finally they returned my call." They've also gotten inbound calls and emails from clients; they've set up appointments and secured placement contracts.

New BUSINESS Was NO ACCIDENT

Ohio Based CSI Complete, a call center serving the insurance industry put together a campaign aimed auto collision repair shops. Their goal was to schedule telephone meetings with the insurance decision makers and ultimately gain new business.

A three part lumpy mail campaign was created to achieve the desired results. The fist mailing consisted of a "message in a bottle" theme that featured a 32oz water bottle imprinted with the logo, contact info and company message. The sales letter was inside the bottle. The letter's headline was "Thirsty for more repair orders?" followed by a sub-head that read "Get ready to drink up! Write more Repair Orders this year and every

year to come when you take action on this message in a bottle."

The second part of the mailing was a bank bag printed with "Put more money in the bank." The headline read "How to write more repair orders while lowering your overhead and improving workplace performance...and you can take that to the bank."

The third part was a metal trash can. Inside the trash can was a crumpled up sales letter. The headline of this third and final letter was "In case you've been throwing away my letters into the trash can, I wanted to do it for you this time. But before you trash my final letter consider that more than 2,500 shops rely on CSI Complete for top rated service. CSI Complete can help you run a more profitable business. But that's just me talking. You be the judge. Take a hard look and you'll see for yourself."

The 3 part promotion generated 42 tele-meetings and 10 new accounts signed up. Total cost of the campaign was $3,500. CSI Complete signed up 10 new accounts at an average of $2,200 for total sales of $22,000. The Return on Investment of 1,000% speaks for itself.

TOYING with Prospects HAS A BIG Payoff

The Service Center is a fulfillment and inventory management company. For their promotion they turned to the power of promotional products to help them reach a very sophisticated target group. Sonnier says "These are very high-end companies, who spend lots of money for fulfillment and related services. They themselves produce and mail out lots of high-end items for their own promotions. The Service Center needed to stand out."

Deciding that an upscale gift might not make much of an impact on them Sonnier chose a unique way to get attention by using toys. "Everyone loves toys. Toys get attention because everyone loves to have fun plus the underlying achievement of associating The Service Center with fun and creativity in the minds of the prospects was a good marketing strategy"

The company used a multi-part mailing with each part featuring a toy that tied in one of the company's strong points: a slinky for flexibility, a candy jar for

storage, a wind up computer for technology and so forth. They also sent out an oversized pair of sunglasses with the message "Are you seeing the big picture?"

So did the promotion work? Sonnier says "It absolutely got the attention we were looking for. Opportunities for new business came in and The Service Center took on several new accounts because of the promotion, including a major retail chain that has become one of the company's top income producers."

An EASY BREEZY WAY to **GENERATE $67,000** In Revenue

Every now and then a client has a product launch that literally screams for a specific promotional product to be tied into the launch. That's exactly what happened when Macromedia, a software company wanted to launch its newest product, Breeze.

Macormedia wanted to convey that Breeze could help top-level executives save time and money, allowing management more time to relax. The brand name and the benefits inspired a tropical beach theme for the promotion.

The promotion was a three part mailing. Each mailing had an accompanying promotional product and was tied into the relaxing tropical beach theme. The promotional products chosen supported the idea of a stress-free, easy breezy work environment.

The first mailing was a zippered coconut inside a box with shredded wood and printed literature that read "No more late nights and lost weekends. With Breeze you can simplify your organization's training and communications, work more efficiently and have time to get a tan."

The second part of the mailing consisted of a desktop fan printed with the Breeze logo. This time the literature read "Keep Cool: no more getting hot and bothered. With Breeze you can train and educate your sales force, channel partners or employee's without breaking a sweat."

The final part of the mailing included a folding beach chair and a request for an appointment. "Sit Here. Let's meet next week and I'll tell you more about Macromedia Breeze solutions. Trust me; you'll be on the edge of your seat."

The multi-part mailings were sent out three days apart to over 200 top level executives. The Macromedia sales staff followed up with phone calls. The promotion secured 50 licensing agreements. The total cost of the campaign was $12,000 and the total revenue generated was $67,000.

Industrial STRENGTH Promotion
Results in 3,900% ROI

They say direct mail is a shotgun approach. Hundreds are sent out in the hopes a few will convert into sales or at the very least a lead. If you've tried sending out inexpensive promotional products to everyone maybe you should rethink the shotgun approach.

Instead of spending a bunch of your entire marketing budget and not really standing out from the competition, why not spend a little more per recipient but have a targeted list of prospects and make the promotion spectacular. You go from the shotgun approach to the highly trained sniper approach.

That's exactly what Canadian company Talbot did with its latest promotion. They built a list of highly valuable prospects and used a series of steel promotional products such as a steel CD case, a steel business portfolio and a steel business card case. They went a step further by packaging all the items in a wood create to add an element of curiosity.

Talbots figured its prospects would appreciate the attention to details and how creatively everything tied into the "Industrial Strength" theme.

The reaction was immediate and somewhat overwhelming. More than half the recipients contacted them which generated six meeting, twelve requests for quotes and over $78,000 in sales.

Not bad for an investment just over $2,000. A Talbot's rep said " We were expecting to at least get our foot in the door but we ended up getting some great business. It came back in spades. We would definitely do a promotion like this again."

Promotion Creates More NEW BUSINESS than SALES CONSULTANT Can Handle

How does the New York Times bestselling author of the book The Ultimate Sales Machine get new sales? I'm talking about incredibly successful sales trainer and consultant Chet Holmes and he uses the power of promotional products!

Holmes says "Basically what we do is pick out our dream clients. The ones that we'd love to work with and we send them one of these little promotional gifts every week for six weeks straight. Then when we call them, they get right on the phone."

Holmes dream list consist of names from the fastest growing INC 500, the entire fortune 1,000, to 200 industry associations and some hand picked smaller businesses. In order to promote his latest book he sent the dream list a multi-part mailing.

First he sent out an orange calculator (keeping with the color of the book) with a sales letter that read "You're going to need an extra calculator to calculate your sales increase, once you apply the concepts in the new book, The Ultimate Sales Machine."

The mailing was followed with a high-liter, a shoe polish kit, a magnifying glass, etc all with a corresponding tag line that referred to his book. Holmes said he received numerous calls not only to buy the book but to schedule consultations. "I'm expecting to get more new business than we can handle. You know in all honesty my time will probably be sold out and I'll just have to keep raising my prices."

If you'd like a free preview of chapter four of The Ultimate Sales Machine simply visit chetholmes.com/book.

Poker Themed Promo Was A WINNING HAND

Citect knows you've got to play the marketing game but the amount they had to play with was limited. They used their limited budget wisely and planned a hotel room drop promotion for a trade show in Vegas. They intended to drive traffic to their trade show booth by holding a drawing for a poker set.

Because the budget was limited they used stock poker-chip printed chocolates to place on pillows in the hotel rooms of attendees. They presented the chocolates with a deck of cards. They packaged the card decks along with marketing collateral about Citect inside a Velcro closure bag that would keep everything neatly inside and make the gifts easy to distribute.

As attendees arrived at their hotel rooms they found the bag with a shinny reflex blue foil imprint with the

tag line "Beat The Odds with Citect" this further supported the theme and reinforced the brands awareness.

Inside they received the branded card decks, the chocolate poker chips and a card that needed to be filled out and dropped off at the Citect booth for a chance to win the poker set.

The promotion was a true winner. Many people stopped by the booth to drop off their cards and thank them for the gift bag. Citect feels they made a lasting impression and the packaging enhanced the perceived value of the brand.

Custom Promotion
Yields 33% RESPONSE RATE

Detweiler, Hershey & Associated isn't your typical accounting firm. When the time came for the firm to introduce new wealth management services to it's client base they wanted to do it with a promotional campaign that would stand out from the usual promotional products that financial services firms tend to give out.

They arrived at this decision because the more typical mailings they had done in the past didn't yield the results they hoped for. The firm in the last few years has been offering clients seminars with little to no response. They would spend hundreds of dollars to send out traditional invitations and produce a very small or no return on investment. This time around the firm went with a much more dramatic approach.

They mailed out a decorative box with full color printed flyers to its 99 largest clients. The marketing literature gave them the details about a free seminar including the benefits of attending and how to register for the seminar. To pique interest a teaser tag line read "Stressed over your finances? Help is just a phone call away."

To further drive the theme and provide recipients with a tangible reminder they included a stress reliever shaped like a cell-phone printed with the firm logo. The firm says the promotion was astounding. A third of the recipients responded to the invitation to attend the seminar, four scheduled appointments and three signed up for the new wealth management service before attending the seminar.

The campaign which cost about $1,800 including shipping and handling more than paid for itself. The firm was so impressed with the results that they did a second campaign using the same format to other clients. This time they placed a branded coaster with the message "We can handle your liquid assets." The firm believes that using the power of promotional products is a solid investment.

It Really Cost
ONLY PENNIES more to HELP REINFORCE
YOUR BRAND AND IMAGE

Even though the recession has put real estate sales on ice Bill Golden of Re/Max Metro Atlanta Citysitde says that promotional products are an important part of his marketing. "I think logoed products are more valuable in a down market, when there's so much competition for business and other agents are less likely to spend the money on such things" Golden adds "I've been in real estate long enough to know that it will rebound and that its just as crucial, if not more, to reinvest in my business during slower periods."

Brian Coeste, president of Coester Appraisal Group says that his company tries to use promotional products in all their marketing efforts. "We use logoed items for all of our marketing. We give away pens, sticky notes, calendars, calculators, and all kinds of things with our logo printed on them to our clients.

WE have found them very effective and well worth the money. We use them when we go into new client's office as a drop off and also to visit existing clients as a reason to stop by."

Denny Grimes, president of Denny Grimes and company says a little creativity goes a long way. I have received a lot of reaction to rubber jar openers because of their "self life and usability."

He says "I give a dozen mugs that say 'You've been mugged by Denny' to the local florist and for $15 I'm able to send the mugs with a floral arrangement inside to my clients and colleagues. People love that. I promote my business every way possible. My staff wears logoed shirts, my coffee is served in logoed mugs and my napkins also have my logo on them. It really cost only pennies more to help reinforce your brand and image."

The BUZZ Lasted For SEVERAL WEEKS

■ t's not possible for a company to achieve it's goals without the dedication of it's employees. Hillcrest Hospital has won several awards from US News and World Report annual ranking of the top
100 hospitals in the country.

To recognize the dedication of their employees they developed an employee recognition program. First the graphics were created and they were tied into some habanero pepper sauce and several spicy grilling sauces.

Employees were divided into three groups. Employees and hospital volunteers were given a habanero sauce in a ful color tube resembling a stick of dynamite. Management received a two bottle pack with habanero sauce and a lime pepper sauce. Lastly administrators and physicians received a three pack with a Cajun sauce, a lime pepper sauce and a peach pepper sauce. All three were printed with the "We're Hot Because of You" message.

A total of 3,500 were distributed with a letter from the hospital CEO. The reaction from employee was incredible. The buzz lasted for several weeks. The employees were thankful for the recognition. It didn't hurt the promotion that the sauces tasted so good.

This kind of promotion can also be used for incentive programs, safety programs, years of service programs and benchmark programs.

Increase BRAND AWARENESS & Push YOUR MESSAGE

Can you think of a better way to grab the attention of dog-lovers than giving them a gift for their beloved canine? That's exactly what Billmae Cottage Suites in Cape May, NJ did to demonstrate that the cottage is dog-friendly. They loved the idea of giving out doggie scarves as the perfect promotional product.

Guest put them on their dogs and as they're walking around the small Victorian sea-side town when they meet other people and when they ask "where are you staying?' and it's visible right there on the dog scarf. The printed scarves increase brand awareness and because they're printed with a tail wagging pup along with the phrase "I stay at the dog friendly Billmae" it pushes the message that they're a dog friendly cottage.

With canine couture being the latest craze thanks in part to celebrities like Paris Hilton it is no surprise that this promotion has gone over so well. The great thing is when guest come back to the Billmae they make sure to bring their doggie scarf.

The Billmae has also given guest other promotional products such as pens, beach bags, sweatshirts and t-shirts. They've also found other ways to promote themselves using the power of promotional products. To create brand awareness they give the restaurants in town Billmae coffee mugs to use when serving dinner coffee. People's reaction is usually "oh look it says Billmae Cottage on it." This is another great way to further promote their brand.

Completely Shocked
When All 350 T-SHIRTS were SOLD OUT IN ONE NIGHT

Most nightclubs, bars and taverns hold special nights to set them apart from the competition and reel in as many people as possible. Just about every bar, tavern or club give out or sells promotional t-shirts.

So when a few bars got together to host an annual multi-venue event called the Turkey Trot. The group was looking for get exposure for their special event and sell a commemorative product to make additional money.

The suggestion was to create a "Turkey Trot" T-shirt that could be sold and would also help promote the event. The T-shirt was costumed designed by a professional graphic artist. The T-shirt was printed on the front with a cocky-looking turkey wearing sunglasses and holding a beer. The back of the T-shirt displayed the logos of all the bars participating in the Turkey Trot.

The promotion was a total success. The bar owners were completely shocked when all 350 T-shirts were sold out in one night. The group reordered T-shirts and sales continued for weeks after the Turkey Trot.

Holiday Gift GENERATES An Additional $100,000 IN SALES FROM TOP CUSTOMERS

As the Holiday season was approaching a Houston, Texas distributor was looking for a gift to give clients that would also help them increase future business. They selected an assortment of gifts that included a classic coaster set, a stainless steel candle set, a shoeshine kit, the Icon action dice set and the Zagat gourmet gift set.

The result was incredible and more than they hoped for. They generated an enormous amount of goodwill and a big increase in business. In the first quarter of the New Year they generated an additional $100,000 in sales from their top customers. When properly planned and thought out the power of promotional products can produce gigantic result even for a small business.

THE Promotion
PAID FOR ITSELF AND THEN SOME

The business world is fierce and small business need to find a creative way to market themselves and standout from the competition. Of all things to use, an imprinted jellyfish yo-yo is what one small business did for its first quarter promotions. The Jellyfish yo-yo went out to hundreds of prospects.

The yo-yo seemed like the prefect way to promote its theme of upward momentum. The yo-yo's sent out with an accompanying postcard that featured of Tulips growing upward. They wanted to convey some upward movement to compliment the yo-yo.

The postcard and the yo-yo were mailed out in a Mylar zip lock mailer. The call to action was a simple "call us for your upcoming needs." They estimate 20% of the recipients contacted them and most became new clients. The first order they received paid for the promotion and then some, which is how they determined that the promotion was a success.

Each Quarter They Recieved Dozens of referrals as A RESULT OF THE PROMOTION

When Exclusively Yours, a consulting firm wanted to increase referrals they turned to the power of promotional products. They created a referral program around the the personalized business approach they practice. They selected items that were soft to create a sense of comfort and warmth.

They launched their referral promotion in early spring when nights are still a bit nippy so they chose a fleece blanket that rolled up with a Velcro strap and handle. The blanket was beautifully embroidered with the company logo. The blankets were sent out whenever they received a referral accompanied with a note that read "Your referral gives us a warm fuzzy feeling."

The referral promotion was so successful they created another theme for the summer. They chose plush bears with the message "Thank you beary much for your referral." And for the winter flu season they created a gift basket with soup packets, imprinted mugs, antibacterial tissues and hand sanitizer gel.

Each quarter they received dozens of referrals as a result of the promotion. One client has been giving them one new referral every week. They estimate $1,000 to $5,000 worth of business from each referral that becomes a new client.

1,644 POTENTIAL New Candidates Were Referred

Referrals cost a lot less than seeking out cold leads. They cost lees because they just fall in your lap. But a good referral is also easier to close on because nothing beats a pre-qualified lead. Referrals can be the life-blood of some businesses.

Why wouldn't you want to generate more referrals? The U.S. Air Force see's the value of referrals so they set out to increase both the quantity and the quality it was getting. The top brass turned to the power of promotional products and came up with a referral campaign named "Get One."

A postcard mailing was created to target the 72,000 Air Force reservists. In order to motivate reservist every time a reservist made a qualified referral, they would get to chose from a variety of promotional products such as a tape measurer, Frisbee or jar opener. If the referral actually signed up for the Air Force the reservist could then pick form a higher level of gifts such as watches, brass coasters, portfolios and calculators.

1,644 potential candidates were referred to the Air Force as a direct result of the "Get One" referral program. The overall quality of the referral candidates was much better than the candidates generated from a basic recruitment drive they signed up 10.3% which is significantly higher than the regular 3% the Air Force has experienced in the past. The "Get One" referral promotion was a huge success for the Air Force.

ABLE TO MEET With 58 Media Contact During The Trade Show

Sumo Glue is an appropriate name for the newest heavy duty, universal glue in the industry. So what better way to create brand recognition than using the image of a Sumo wrestler and that's exactly what they did to launch the new glue product.

In order to convey the strength of the product they used a Sumo stress reliever to send out with their media kits. They sent out media kits along with the Sumo stress relievers to media outlets that were likely to attend the National Hardware show in Las Vegas. The response was better than expected and they were able to meet with 58 media contacts during the show and introduce them to the new product.

The Sumo stress relievers were mentioned in almost every conversation they had with the media contacts. They served as the perfect reminders to not only stop by the booth but also that Sumo Glue was the newest product on the market and that they would muscle out the competition. Using this promotional product not only made the promotion memorable but it also helped give the product a personality.

BREAKING THROUGH
The Media Clutter

One might think that the Panda bear which only eats bamboo would be an odd choice to promote a new beef entrée at a restaurant. But it all makes sense when the restaurant is Panda Express, a Chinese fast food chain with more the 1,000 stores nationwide.

Panda Express sent out a teaser promotion to restaurant and marketing media several weeks before announcing their latest menu item. They sent the media contacts a plain white box containing two plush pandas labeled Tom-Tom and Eddie. An accompanying printed card read "Experience Pandamonium at Panda Express and suggested they check their in boxes for "Big, beefy news."

What could be more cute and lovable than plush panda bears? The choice was a natural fit to promote the new Beijing Beef entrée. The plush pandas made this a comprehensive promotion. "Media editors and reporters said they loved the panda bears. It certainly broke through the clutter and we are still getting results."

Promotion Delivered MORE BUSINESS than Paul COULD KEEP UP WITH

Mortgage office, Paul Walsh quickly started to see customer service fall apart after the mortgage company he worked for was bought out. Paul knew things we're heading in the wrong direction and it was time to abandon ship. But Paul didn't want to lose the customer base that he worked so hard to build. He needed a way to let his customers know that he would still be offering his services.

It took Paul a few months to find a top notch company to work with. And now came the time to inform his customers that he was with a new company and ready to serve hi customers. The promotional product selected for the task was a postcard magnet featuring a full color caricature of Paul.

The headline on the postcard read "What's different about this picture?" And the subhead said "The face looks familiar, but has the company changed?" The caricature presented Paul in a unique way beyond the typical mortgage broker picture on the business card. The caricature gave Paul personality and reminded the recipients that they know Paul and his friendly, professional level of service.

The magnet postcard was planned as the first step in a multi-step direct mail campaign. After the overwhelming response Paul put part two on hold. The first part of the promotion delivered more business than Paul could keep up with.

GENERATED 30% MORE
Over Previous Months

A name change is never easy. But getting nine bank branches along with all of its employees and thousands of customers to embrace the name change makes it even harder. However with the power of promotional products the challenge became an opportunity for Downingtown National Bank (DNB) when they changed their name to DNB First. The bank leveraged the name change and turned it into a customer appreciation event that created new business for the bank.

DNB has a 144 year history in Chester County, PA. The promotion was to gain exposure and generate brand awareness for the local bank among its customers, staff and the public at large regarding the new name, logo and image of the independent bank. The promotion evolved beyond brand recognition and also drove new Cds, checking and savings accounts.

The bank used 15 different promotional products including banners and balloons printed with the new gray and burgundy DNB first logo. They were placed in branch lobbies during the first week of the campaign. They also distributed to their employees gift bags containing a magnetic name badge, a burgundy polo shirt, a mug filled with burgundy and gray M&Ms, a mouse pad, pens and a note cube all imprinted with the new DNB First logo.

Customer who visited the branch during the first week of the promotion also received pens and note cubes. Through out the promotion customers also received as gifts can koozies, bottled water and jar openers which were tied into "opening" a new account.

Customers who signed up for a new Cd, checking account or saving account received an insulted cooler bag filled with more logoed promotional products. Overall 5,000 of each product were given out to customers and employees. They generated 30% more new Cd, checking accounts and savings accounts over previous months.

Elizabeth Cook, assistant VP of Marketing for DNB First attributed the success of the campaign to the well thought out selection of promotional products. She says "The gifts to employees made them feel they were part of the name change and the excitement associated with it. The items we gave away to customers reinforced all the other activities going on. They helped create more awareness and gave tellers a chance to talk up the new logo."

An INNOVATIVE WAY TO USE The Power Of PROMOTIONAL PRODUCTS

What could be better than snatching up a concert t-shirt of your favorite band? Well how about snatching up a USB Bracelet upload with the live concert you just attended. That was one of the best selling items at the Matchbox Twenty concert. Rob Thomas, Matchbox Twenty lead singer said in an interview with USA Today "I just think it's neat. It's really fun knowing how much is inside that USB wristband. It's not just the songs but also behind the scenes footage, wallpapers and desktop icons are also loaded onto the bracelet."

The company behind this revolutionary idea is Access Today. The bracelet cost $30 which is the same price of a concert t-shirt and can be purchased at the concert or at the Matchbox Twenty website. The wristband is an innovative way to use the power of promotional products to get the songs into the fans hands.

Not only is there a high demand for interactive experiences from the consumers but it also beats getting a bootleg copy of the concert. The product also offers advertisers the opportunity to include a sponsor message or imprint a logo on the wristband itself.

The Mailing was a BIG SUCCESS!

Luzers Archive, a magazine that showcases print ad campaigns and TV commercials was looking for an out-of-the-box way to promote itself to the management and creative directors at U.S advertising agencies. So how they used the power of promotional products to help increase brand awareness and sell subscriptions to the magazine.

The magazine needed a creative direct mail campaign. They needed a direct mailer that would get creative people that have seen it all to open it, that would reinforce that the Archive is the ultimate idea generator for creative agencies. The mailer would direct people to the web site to learn more about the magazine subscription.

They came up with mailing an expandable sponge in the shape of a light bulb. The shape would easily make the connection between the magazine and generating ideas. The increase the open rate they placed the item in a clear envelope so that the recipient knew what was inside before they even opened it. Ad agency people are very hard to impress but the sponge broke through the clutter.

"The mailing was a big success. We've been getting calls from agencies who love the sponge and want to use it for their own promotion." There is a lesson here for marketers…don't overlook flat, easy to mail items such as magnets, mouse pads, air fresheners, temporary tattoos, etc. Just because it's flat doesn't mean your response rate will be.

INUNDATED With CALLS AND EMAILS

The St. Louis Regional Clean Air Partnership was created to bring awareness to air quality and to encourage people in the area to help reduce air pollution. The partnership typically sends out press releases and emails to promote its cause. But when they choose to add the power of promotional products to its marketing mix they were inundated with calls and emails.

The press release informed the media that if people went to their website www.cleanairstlouis.com they could sign up to receive daily air quality forecast and those that signed up would receive a free insulated lunch bag filled with other promotional items such as a stadium cup, pencils, pens and a notepad all imprinted with the partnership logo.

The choice of insulted lunch bag fits in perfectly with the clean air message because they encourage people to pack a lunch instead of driving during lunch as a way to cut back on emissions.

The Power Of Promotional Products
DREW THEM IN... POCKET PC'S
MICROSOFT SOLD OVER 10,000

When Microsoft wanted to amp up sales of its Pocket PC through national retail chains they created a six week campaign titled "Demo Days." The campaign involved educating its reps. Retail brand support and motivating both retailers and consumers.

Microsoft licked off "Demo Days" with a two day seminar to educate the 225 reps that would act as spokespeople in retail outlets through out the country. The reps not only received training but they also walked away with Microsoft branded backpacks stuffed with notepads and pens that they could use while on-site giving demos at the retail level. To further reinforce the brand during the two day event they also had bottles of water and M&M's with the Microsoft logo. To create a team atmosphere between the 225 reps wore blue button down shirts beautifully embroidered with the Microsoft logo.

To push the brand at the retail level they created POP displays. Store managers received branded Swiss Army knives. To reinforce the brand all 225 reps wore their blue button down shirts while giving live demonstrations to consumers.

To further motivate consumers they handed out magnets and pens with the Microsoft logo. Marjorie Cooper, a marketing professor at Baylor University says "This was a good promotion because it engaged all of the supply chain links-reps, retailers and consumers. The wide range of supporting promotional products increased the likelihood that recipients would be drawn into participation in the campaign."

It's without a doubt that the power of promotional products drew them in because in the six week period Microsoft sold over 10,000 Pocket PC's.

Creating A $9 - $11 ROI PER GIFT

Country Inn & Suites emphasizes a home-like atmosphere. They are the leaders in mid-scales hotels. The brand see's its target demographics as families. For the last several years the company has done a summer promotion that centers around a kids summer movie release.

For this year the marketing team partnered with Warner Brothers for the debut of The Ant Bully. They created The Ant Bully Family Package which featured a special family room rate, free stay for the kids and an imprinted backpack filled with promotional gifts.

The kids imprinted backpack came filled with an activity book, a bag tag, a game, various snacks and a pair of swimming goggles.

Barbare Radatz the senior marketing director said "The package boosted revenue. If we look at what a regular room rates would bring in versus what this package would bring, its $12-$14 more per room. What is really the driver is the value   behind the fact that it's tied into the Ant Bully movie.

By partnering with companies such asWarner Brothers and Jolly Time Popcorn, they kept cost down to around $4 per family gift pack…creating a $9-$10 ROI per room.

MISSION Accomplished!

This past winter the Newton Athletic Club was looking for a practical but unique thank you gift to give its members. The Newton Athletic Club offers wellness programs for adults and kids as well as an onsite spa, salon and daycare.

Between the daycare center and the kids' wellness programs the club has hundreds of kids. During the winter months that adds up to a whole lot of runny noses. The tissue cup dispenser was the perfect promotional product for the gym to give its members during the winter months. And the tissue cup design which is meant to fit in cars cup holder made it a practical and unique gift.

The tissue cup showed members that they gym cared about its them because they understood that during Flu season people were always reaching for a tissue whether in the gym or in the car. It's a sign that they went the extra mile to help their members. They gave out 1,000 branded tissue cups to members as they checked in. The objective of the promotion was to create goodwill and loyalty among the members of the club during flu season...Mission Accomplished!

GREAT JOB OF
Increasing Traffic
TO THE BOOTH

Paradise Spa needed a way to increase traffic to their booth during the upcoming home show. The hot tub dealer wanted to use a gift to give to attendees that visited their booth. Paradise Spa wanted a promotional product that was useful, grabbed attention and would tie in to their new stress free maintenance program.

After presenting numerous options Paradise went with idea of a toy slinky. They choose the mini toy slinky in a variety of metallic colors printed with the Paradise Spa logo. The spring toy has an appeal that covers all age groups.

Paradise Spa gave them out to people who stopped by their booth and listened to a quick sales presentation about Paradise Spa. Most people attending the Home Show are families with children people like the fact that they received a kid friendly item. Paradise Spa sales reps benefited from the kid friendly item because the toy kept the kids busy while the parents checked out the different spa and listened to the presentation given by the Paradise staff working the booth.

The power of promotional products did a great job of increasing traffic to the booth. It seems that everyone at the show wanted to get their hands on the toy springs. "When other attendees and kids saw the toy springs they all wanted to get one so they headed to the Paradise Spa booth."

An Increase In Sales
OF 35%

The increasing use of digital cameras caused sales at the photo department of national pharmacy chain Walgreens to plummet. Walgreens drastically needed a way to find a way to bring in digital camera user to the store for photo printing services. They needed to not only bring them in but they needed to get them coming back.

After many brainstorming session Walgreens was presented with several ideas. After reviewing the suggested ideas Walgreens decided to use the USB Flash Drive to bring in digital camera users.

The USB Flash Drives were sent out to customers in the stores database along with instructions on how to download photos from a digital camera or computer onto the flash drive. As an incentive they also included a coupon for 12 free 4x6 prints.

The promotion was a huge success for Walgreens photo department. Within the first two weeks the photo department had an increase in sales of 35%. Customers were thrilled with the flash drive and excited about how convenient it was to download their pictures and having them printed at their local Walgreens.

Walgreens says that people came back over and over again with their branded flash drive to order prints.

Promotion Motivates 65% of the employees to complete The On-Line Training

After launching HP Invent, Hewlett-Packard wanted to persuade it's 400 call center reps to go to the website and complete on-line training course for the new product. In order to motivate its reps they created an incentive promotion with a prize of two Xbox game consoles. The only problem was that employees still needed to be directed to the web site to learn about the opportunity.

The power of promotional products came to the rescue. A high tech promotional product was proposed to match the tech-savy HP employees. Each employee worked in a cubicle so there was limited real estate to work with therefore wireless programmable mouse was the perfect item.

The programmable wireless mouse was a great way to captivate the recipients. By programming the scroll wheel/click action the HP web site was just a click away. HP didn't have to worry about promoting a web address and recipients didn't have to remember the URL. This was a seamless way to convey essential information about the promotion with minimal hassles.

Basically every employee received the mouse inside a box printed with a full color graphic with the message: "click...and Win!" Once they opened the box they found the HP branded mouse and the install disc.

The contest lasted three weeks. During the three week period 65% of the employees that received the package followed the mouse to the on-line training and completed the course. As a result of the effectiveness of the promotion HP rolled out the campaign to its four other call centers.

MORE SALES PEOPLE
THAN EXPECTED
Hit Their Quota

Countrywide Home Loans used the power of promotional products to motivate its nationwide sales staff to hit their new revenue goals. Countrywide understood that the new quotas were higher but the reward of a vacation to the beautiful island of Puerto Rico was a great incentive.

The next step was to find a creative way to deliver the message. Countrywide needed to bring attention to the big reward. They tie into the success of the "Survivor" realty show. They choose promotional products that would tie in with the "Survivor" theme.

The logoed products were packaged in a hallowed out and split coconut with a zipper. Inside the coconut recipients found a compass, a flashlight, a lip balm, sunscreen and a brochure announcing the new Countrywide sales incentive program.

The feedback from the sales staff was instant. The promotion was truly a success as more sales people than anticipated hit their new quota and won the vacation to Puerto Rico.

THE PROMOTION was a winner with OVER 76%
Of Their Salespeople
Hitting Their Quotas

During the cold winter months a sales incentive contest offering a free cruise to Miami and the Bahamas can be irresistible. The key to having a successful sales incentive contest is to conjure up positive thoughts of the destination and keep the positivity going.

The power of promotional products used ass teasers is a great way to promote a sales contest and keep the positive message going through out the contest period. "The goal was to keep motivating their salespeople through continuous promotional mailings for example sunglasses, sunscreen and other beach items."

The company also sent its 300 sales people frames with a unique antique map design to help give the promotion a travel-like theme. The frames were sent with a picture of the Bahamas in it to help conjure up positive imagery and further motivate its sales force to hit their quotas.

The promotion was a winner with over 76% of their salespeople hitting their quotas and attending the cruise to the Bahamas.

The Message Spread As Quickly As A WILD FIRE

The number one soda brand on the market wanted to find a way to let consumers know just how much Coke Zero tastes like regular Coke except without the calories. When Coca Cola first launched Coke Zero they struggled to get the message out. But when they came up with "877-Sue-Zero" the message spread as quickly as a wild fire.

They also created the fictional law firm Covet &Yourminy (pronounced covet your money). They ran ads two sleazy looking lawyers that egged consumers to go to Suezero.com. There they could submit detail as to how Coke Zero has confused them in exchange for a taste confusion kit.

The taste confusion kit included a cover letter and a can Koozie with the law firm's logo on it and a coupon for a free Coke and A Coke Zero. The cover letter from lead attorney Yourminy read "Dear prospective plantiff: We have received your taste infringement case, and it is strong. Really strong. We can almost picture you at the helm of your own 60 foot sailboat."

Coca Cola choose a can koozie because it helped make the story more about the product and brought attention to the product itself. They were right on the money because the product got the attention of media outlets across the country. USA Today wrote "Coke finally scores another win with its Coke Zero promotion." 14,500 taste confusion kits were mailed out and over 17,000 calls were made to "888-Sue-Zero.

Close MORE SALES On The First Visit

You'd think that when the Metal Depot created a promotional campaign they would be targeting men and not kids. The Metal Depot understands that when ordering a metal roof it's a detailed conversation. You need to have your attention on the details without worrying about little Johnny running around.

The Metal Depot put together a "busy kids kit" to keep the kids busy while the parents shopped for their new metal roof. The "Busy Kids Kit" includes a flying disk, house shaped pencils, yo-yo stress balls and a kids t-shirt.

Metal Depot basically hands out to the parents when they come in and they've also set up a little table and chairs for the kids along with some coloring books and crayons. Keeping the promotional products for kids has allowed Metal Depot to close more sales on the first visit and has decrease the amount of follow up need to close a deal.

TOTAL REVENUE
During The Four Week Promotion was over $2.0 Million

How do you increase sales of a PC game by 20%? You create a gift with purchase that would go on to become a collector's item. That's exactly what they did for the release of Star Wars Jedi Knight. With a target audience of 15 to 35 year old males the item had to reflect the hi-tech image of the Star Wars brand. Not only did the item need to be cool and hip it also had to have mass appeal to the huge age range.

The goal was to achieve a 50% sell through at the retail level within the first four weeks of the games release. The gift with purchase chosen was a flashing light wand that simulated the Star Wars Light Saber. The mini Light Saber would be packaged with the game disc inside a tin box. The metal tin further conveyed the games futuristic image. The tin box was also to become a collector's item and would be used afterwards for storage.

The gift with purchase promotion generated over $750,000 in revenue in just the first week. 75% of the collector's tin sets were sold out within the four weeks of the promotion. Total revenue during the four week promotion was over $2.0 million. The game held the number one spot for games sales for just over two months. Lucas Art believes the gift with purchase along with the packaging had a lot to do with the success of the games launch.

The promotion also created long term brand recognition. As for the mini Light Saber, well it continues to be used and has become a staple item for all Lucas Art Star Wars events, conventions and tradeshows.

THE MOST
Visible Brand
TWO-DAY TRADESHOW
During The

How do you get trade show-goers to not only come to your booth for a free tote bag but also get them to use carry your promotional tote bag everyday they walk the tradeshow floor? You create a contest.

That's exactly what the TRG group did. The contest worked like this: TRG Group staff handed out 5,000 tote bags embroidered with the TRG Group logo to everyone that stopped by their booth.  Each bag had a numbered hang tag on it. Out of the 5,000 tote bags five hundred had a number that matched another bag. If the recipients could find their match on the show floor, both numbers holders could return to the TRG Group booth and claim a free iPod.

TRG Group had people searching the tradeshow floor for their match. "People told us they had up to 15 people come up to them looking for their number to see if they were a match. We even had some people put the tag in a more visible place like hanging it from their name tag so others would be sure to see their number" says Andrew Spellman, TRG vice president of sales.

Over the next two days a number of people found their match and won an iPod and the tote bag was the center of attention at the tradeshow. "Most importantly," Spellman notes "the majority of people brought their totes back for day two of the show. The promotion was a huge success."

The TRG Group logo was the most visible brand during the two-day tradeshow. This promotion created a priceless increase in brand awareness for the TRG Group.

A Need TO KEEP UP with Our Competitors

We've all heard of on-the-job training but I bet you haven't heard of on-the-job marketing. I think the term was created by creative-staffing firm The Boss Group. The agency gives the candidates it place plenty a whole bunch of Boss Group logoed promotional products to keep handy in the offices where they'll be working.

Jenna Stone, director of marketing and communications, says that Boss staffers frequently work alongside other people that were placed by a competing staffing agency. Jenna says "we've even had a case where one of our staffers sent us pictures of his cubicle with all of our items and a picture of his neighbor's cubicle with the competitor's items. So there does seem to be a need to keep up with our competitors."

The Boss Group is currently using a branded gift bag that holds an oversized mug, some translucent pens, and notepad all branded with the agency logo. Jenna says "We wanted something that stayed on the desk, that was functional and that was sort of simple…something they're actually going to use."

The sales team also uses the gift bags when going out to meet with new prospects. The promotional products also give the sales team an occasion to get a visit with an existing client. They say that they're bringing them something and want to drop it off and that enables them to get face time with clients.

In Less Than
SIX MONTHS,
Appleone EXPERIENCED
Noticeable Growth

Appleone Employment Service was looking for a way to quickly expand its business. Appleone wanted to place emphasis on two main areas: 1) the quality of the employees they place and 2) the range of services it provides. With a little help from the power of promotional products they did just that.

Appleone used a selection of promotional products that would help them increase the visibility of their brand. The promotion consisted of two parts. One part to show their quality and another part to highlight the additional services they offer.

In the first part, whenever they placed an employee in a position they gave the employee a "launch Kit" which consisted of a tote bag with an imprinted pen and an imprinted water bottle. "As placed employees used the items through out the day, the Appleone name became more and more recognizable and associated with the staffing-service employee. " Says Lewis. "As the workers continued to excel, the Aplleone brand became synonymous with a highly reliable staffing source."

The second part of the promotion consisted of bi-monthly mailings to human resource managers in their customer database. Each mailing featured a different color tumble imprinted with the Appleone logo along with a fact sheet about their different services such as accounting, payroll, and information technology.

Lewis reports that the company saw excellent results from the two pronged promotion. "In less than six months, Appleone experienced noticeable growth in their overall staffing and service levels." The campaign was a huge success-so successful that they plan to expand the existing program next year to include companies not currently in their database.

How GOOGLE Built A WINNING PROMOTION

When the search engine powerhouse known as Google had an idea for launching its 2008 "Build Big, Think Big" marketing campaign the power of promotional products stepped up to the challenge creating a unique promotional campaign.

Google's goal for the campaign was to reach from medium sized businesses to high level executives at large corporations with it's "Build Big, Think Big" promotion. The message Google wanted to promote to its clients was that they had a complete "suite" of products to offer.

When you think of search engines you can't help to think of Google but they wanted to spread the word that it has the capability to support clients in a variety of business needs. Google chose to send out oversized Lego blocks to it's clients printed with phrases such as "Video Ads" and "Global Reach". To truly harness the power of promotional products Google wanted something that would stay behind long after the promotion was over.

After some brainstorming the idea to package the printed blocks in the metal toolbox came to life. For Google it wasn't enough to simply send out the promotional blocks in a regular box. They anted something that would stand out, grab attention and that people would continue to use.

The marketing campaign thanks to the power of promotional products was a huge success for Google. About 700 of the 4,000 packages created were sent out to high profile companies like Maxim Magazine and Harley Davidson.

Apparently when you mix toys with business it equals a whole lot of success. When creative minds turn to the power of promotional products they come up with winning campaigns.

It Ended The Rumors
SPREAD FROM WITHIN AND FROM COMPETITORS

When a company goes thru a merger and acquisition the rumors start flying. And when the rumors start flying it can be bad for employee moral because and leaves clients feeling uneasy and out of the loop.

CSI, heating and ventilation control systems manufacturer, wanted to make sure moral wouldn't plummet during its impending acquisition. CSI was looking for a way to keep employees motivated and clients positive about the transition.

CSI decided that it needed a partner with deeper pockets in order to handle the volume from larger account. CSI had been family owned and operated for decades and they wanted to reassure its employees and clients that they weren't just looking for a way to cash out, line their pockets and leave the company.

CSI went in with a team approach and created a theme of a rely race. The concept was that the baton was being passed from CSI to TAC. They conveyed the analogy that CSI had done its part through the first leg of the relay race and this was the last leg of the race and in order to win the race they had to pass the baton.

CSI distributed to its 300 top employees and clients a real track and field baton on a clear desktop base printed with both company logos and a message that read "Mastering the Game." They explained the acquisition, why it was going to happen and the benefits for all involved.

"It ended the rumors spread from within and from competitors and thoroughly explained the move. And the product fit in so well with the 'passing the baton' analogy…it really was a perfect campaign."

Promotional Products
enhance BRAND AWARENESS & BRAND LOYALTY

Some companies think that because they're the leaders in their market place that they don't need to create brand awareness. But smart companies understand that advertising helps them maintain and build a deeper connection between the brand and the customer.

A good example of how to continue building a brand even when you're the market leader is Beneteau, a manufacturer of sailboats. The company has five factories in France as well as a presence in the U.S with a manufacturing operation in Marion, South Carolina and a sales office in Charleston.

The brand has a strong brand loyalty from avid sailors and chances are they've sailed one, owned one or still do. Beneteau owners tend to stay loyal to the brand. Despite the widespread brand loyaltyBeneteau USA continues to promote itself. One of the ways they continue to market the brand is thru the use of branded promotional products. "We have an entire apparel line with caps, shirts and jackets," says a company spokesperson as well as items like can cozies, key tags, coolers floating sunglass cases and other items are regularly given out at events.

Once a year they further take advantage of the power of promotional products by sending out custom imprinted lapel pins to all owners and key suppliers. The brand hopes that they'll collect the lapel pins and display them on caps and jackets. It began the promotion four years ago and have started a Beneteau tradition. The company tag line "The Sea Demands The Best" is always imprinted on the pins.

They mail out 5,000 custom pins a year attached to happy New Year's card. The success of the promotion is hard to measure thought many owners are seen wearing their Beneteau pins while attending events says the company spokesperson. "They like the pins very much. The pins enhance owner loyalty. They're a unique keepsake from Beneteau."

Promotional Products
STIMULATE SALES

With the economy in a recession, ticket sales for sporting events are down. Those who invest n season tickets should really be rewarded by the team they support.

The Los Angeles Kings hockey team wanted a thank you gift to encourage season ticket sales from loyal fans. The team selected several promotional products packaged inside a Los Angles Kings branded gym bag.

The gift bag simulated season ticket sales and was a huge hit with loyal Kings fans. Several season ticket holders called or wrote to thank them for the gift.

Very Effective Promotion
to boost SALES & AWARENESS

CosmoGirl magazine partnered up with nationwide pharmacy chain Rite Aid for a very effective promotion to boost sales and awareness for its branded CosmoGirl brand makeup.

The promo was aimed at 15 year old girls. The firm used a hot pink and black zebra stripped self standing frame that also doubled as a mirror printed with the Cosmo Girl logo. The back was magnetic so it was the perfect promotional product to use in school lockers. The promotional item conveyed an image of being cool.

The promotion titled "Makeover Mania" was targeted at the energy of teenage girl's passion for makeup, hair and fashion. They also created signage for the Rite Aid stores that encouraged girls to check out the Cosmo Girl makeup line. The frame/mirror was a gift with purchase. The girls had to send in the original store receipt to receive the gift. The promotion achieved its goals and to date over 5,000 frames have been sent out.

Promotional Kits Placed In
OVER 2,000 SALONS

Francesca Vietor, co-founder of the grassroots organization 1,000 Flowers wanted to make sure single women across the country were going out to vote.

"We were trying to figure out where we could target young women and where they hung out. They don't have sewing circle anymore, so we were looking for a place where women can have leisurely time to talk about the issues in a supporting sisterly atmosphere. And we found it's while they're waiting for their appointments or for their mails or hair to dry. That's when they have to time to fill out a form." Says Victoria and we agree since salons are abundant in every neighborhood.

Victoria says "we're targeting single women because we learned that 22 million single women didn't vote in the last election and 16 million weren't even registered voters. So we decided to do something about it." A promotional program called "Adopt-a-Salon" was created to recruit volunteers to provide their neighborhood salons with a display and promotional products free from 1,000 Flowers.

The display along with the free promotional products were named "Beauty Kits" and consisted of a large counter display with postcards about the five reasons to vote and nail files printed with catch phrases such as "Don't let this election be a nail biter", "shape the oval office" and "File your complaint." The promotional kits also contained voter registration forms.

The promotion was a huge success and without the use of the promotional "Beauty Kits" they would have never gotten placement in over 2,000 salons across the country.

The First Weekend Drew In More Than 10,000 ATTENDEES

Every summer across the country before most are thinking about football, players are reporting to training camps to prepare for the upcoming football season. While a few diehard fans attend the training camps the numbers are not very high. However the New York Jets were determined to get fans fired up this years training camp.

The Jets employed a street team to distribute Jets logoed promotional items at high traffic location through out the city. The promotion was created to get people fired up and thinking about Jets football before the season started.

The street teams gave out Jets temporary tattoos, Jets bracelets, Jets water bottles, Jets playbooks and schedule magnets. They selected premiums they felt the fans would want to hang on to. Water bottles have a high perceived value and the tattoos and bracelets would allow fans to show their support for the Jets. The magnets have a long life span once put up on a refrigerator and would help keep the Jets top of mind all season long.

Well the promotion was a summer blockbuster and the Jets definitely got the attention and support of their fans. Attendance at the summer training camp tripled this years compared to previous years. The first weekend drew in more than 10,000 attendees.

THESE PRODUCTS Really Help!

Advertisers are the life blood of any magazine. But in order to have advertisers they need to consistent readers and preferably loyal subscribers year after year. However when it comes to subscriptions literary magazines fall short because they cater to a specialized niche in the magazine market.

The Missouri Review knew this when they wanted to increase its subscribers. "The promotion was to up our web subscription sales for a three year deal, because three year deals are always better for a magazine than a single year subscription," says Kris Somerville, Missouri Review marketing director. "Then we don't have to sign everyone back up every single year."

The Missouri Review understands the power of promotional products. For several years, usually four or five times a year, they've been using promotional products to increase response rates to subscription promotions.

"We believe if you give out a good product that seems too good to be true, people tend to subscribe," adds Somerville. "This audience doesn't like cheap trinkets. What they want is quality and functionality."

This year the Missouri Review selected several products which they offered depending on the subscription package. The products included a T-shirt, tote bag and coffee mug all branded with the magazine logo.

"It's been a success we've just been re-ordering the same products every three months and we're getting an average of one Web subscriber a day. We currently have a circulation of 5,000. For a literary magazine that's a high number. These products really help with that."

THREE QUARTERS Of The SALES TEAM MEET Their Quotas

Nokia turned to the power of promotional products to kick off an annual incentive program for its sales team in an effort to help them reach their sales quotas and increase revenue.

The theme of the promotion revolved around a Zen image. They had posters printed with the image of a person meditating on a rock beach. The perfect product to carry the message was a smooth, printed river rock packaged in a 100% cotton drawstring bag.

The message printed on the rock "Rock solid internet security for absolute peace of mind" tied into the posters and the Zen rock beach theme. Three quarters of the sales team meet their quotas and advanced to the next level of the multi-tiered incentive promotion. The incentive promotion was a success for Nokia and produced very good results.